The
Cookie
Cracker

150 Unusual and
Mouth-Watering Temptations
by Anne Lanigan

MW01047842

Marcia Bere,
Donna Falgarelli

In Great Britain: Book Sales Ltd., 78 Newman Street, London W1P 3LA.
In Canada: Gage Trade Publishing, P.O. Box 5000, 164 Commander Blvd., Agincourt, Ontario M1S 3C7.
In Japan: Quick Fox, 2-13-19 Akasaka, Tamondo Bldg., Minato-ku, Tokyo 107.

Book and cover design: Barry L.S. Mirenburg
Cover photograph: David Frazier
Book illustrations: Michael Emerson

Contents

Introduction

As you can imagine, this cookbook was a lot of fun to work on. When I was working on my earlier cookbook, *The Yogurt Gourmet*, many people said they didn't want to taste the test recipes because they didn't like yogurt. With this project, a hungry horde devoured each and every batch of cookies. They even loved the parsnip cookies because they didn't know the ingredients.

There has been some discussion lately about the psychological reasons for the proliferation of cookie shops and the great increase in cookie consumption. One theory holds that in a time of uncertainty, cookies offer comfort and reassurance, reminding us of childhood. Others hold that this is merely an extension of the American habit of snacking. In any case, whether any or all of the above are factors, it is indisputable that people *love* cookies.

What are cookies and crackers? The dictionary informs us that the word "cookie" comes from the Dutch or Flemish *koekje*, meaning small cake; the Dutch word for cake is *koek*. What is a cookie to us is a biscuit to an Englishman, Australian or Canadian. As to crackers, *Oxford English Dictionary* defines one as a "thin, hard biscuit" and notes that the term is used mostly in the United States.

In view of the fact that everyone seems to love cookies, it seemed to me that a cookbook about them would be welcome, since homemade cookies are vastly superior to store-bought ones. During the time that I was working on this book, everyone to whom I mentioned the project reacted with enthusiasm and delighted anticipation. Many people offered their treasured and favorite recipes, and you will find some of them included in this collection.

I believe that cookies have an emotional appeal for us, apart from their tasting good. They remind us of the simple pleasures of childhood — cookies and lemonade on a hot day, or cookies and hot chocolate on a frosty day; cookies with icy cold milk as a bedtime snack, or cookies with hot tea on a cold and rainy afternoon; cookies with ice cream for a special dessert; cookies as an embellishment for a simple fruit dessert; cookies with fruit juice for a midmorning snack. And in later years, boxes of cookies sent to us when we were away at school or camp.

As to our well-known "sweet tooth" it does not seem to be the result of conditioning as many people think. Researchers at the Monell Chemical Senses Center in Philadelphia have established a preference for sweets in newborn babies. They theorize that this evolved in early man so that he was attracted by fruits and vegetables which provided him with important nutrition.

It is the elimination of any nutritive ingredients that gives many sweets a bad name and leads to their being described as "empty calories." It is possible, however, to make a sweet cookie which includes nutritious ingredients, such as vegetables, soybeans, soy flour, coconut, raisins and nuts. The texture of shredded coconut can also be achieved by using shredded raw vegetables, such as carrots, parsnips, zucchini, etc., which will be lower in calories than the coconut.

Crackers are a nonsweet snack, and there are many varieties of them. Although the plain soda cracker does not seem to turn out well in the home oven, there are many other delicious crackers whose good flavor can be enhanced with ingredients that possess sound nutritional value.

Baking cookies and crackers gives a cook the satisfaction of making something good, and they are easy to make. They don't require the time involved in making bread or some of the skills needed for fancy pastry. They're quick to bake, the equipment needed is minimal and inexpensive, and the gratification is almost immediate (just let them cool slightly!). So have fun — and bake away!

Equipment

Aluminum Foil

Aluminum foil is a tremendous help when making cookies. Use it shiny side up. It is indispensable when making very thin or fragile cookies as you do not have to try lifting the cookies off the sheet after they are baked. Gently ease the foil over a rolling pin and the cookies will detach themselves from the foil as it becomes rounded. The foil can be wiped clean with a paper towel and used again.

When making a large batch of cookies, cut sheets of foil to fit the cookie sheets. Form the cookies on as many sheets of foil as are necessary and slip the cookie sheet under the foil. As each batch is finished, remove the baked cookies on their foil sheet and slip the cookie sheet under the next batch. You do not have to butter the foil.

Cookie Cutters

Cookie cutters come in many shapes and sizes. Try to get the tin ones, which are sharper than either plastic or aluminum. Dip the cutter into flour or confectioners' sugar as necessary to prevent sticking. If dough should harden on a cookie cutter, soak cutter in warm water and detergent to loosen the dough. Never scour cutters with abrasives, for these can scratch and gouge them.

When cutting out cookies, start at the outer edge of the dough, cut the cookies as close to each other as possible, and work toward the center of the dough. For more on cutting, see Pastry Wheel.

Cookie Press

Some people seem to like using a cookie press but I am not one of them. Cookie dough to be used in a press must be fairly stiff and requires more flour than is desirable for most cookie doughs. Because of this stiff dough, cookies from the press have very little variety in texture and tend to taste alike. I much prefer using a pastry bag, which is easier to control and clean, or cookie cutters.

Cookie Sheets

The sheet should be flat without a rim or with a rim on two sides only. The rim makes for ease in handling but is not absolutely necessary. Shiny aluminum is the best material — the heavier the better. Measure your oven to determine the proper size cookie sheet; it should be 2 inches shorter and 2 inches narrower than your oven to allow 1 inch on all sides for proper air circulation. A standard sheet measures 12 by 15½ inches. Try to get one measuring about ⅛ inch in thickness (it will weigh 24 ounces) rather than the more common one which is only about 1/16 inch thick (weighing 12 ounces). It is possible to get sheets cut to your specifications (see Sources, p. 224). A heavier sheet prevents scorching and is a better conductor of heat. The black steel pans and the nonstick ones tend to cook the bottoms too fast.

If there are not enough cookies to fill the last sheet, use a cake pan upside down or the removable bottom from a quiche pan.

Cooling Racks

You will need more than one cooling rack, preferably made of wire. Most cake or cookie cooling racks are made of parallel wires but the better ones are made with the wires intersecting at right angles to form a grid.

The average cooling rack has legs that are only ½ inch high, which does not permit proper circulation of air and can result in soggy cookies. The best solution is to place the rack on a cake pan or loaf pan, thus providing the necessary elevation. I have a large oval wire tray with a 1½ inch rim. I very often use it inverted as an extra cooling rack.

Docker

A docker is a gadget that looks like a miniature tennis court roller that is studded with thin sharp nails. It is used to prick holes in cracker dough and shortbread to keep them flat. It is a great help for other baking as well, such as for pricking pie shells.

Electric Mixer

Although most cookies can be made by hand, an electric mixer is a boon in the kitchen, particularly when a recipe calls for 20 minutes of beating. Mixers are also time-savers. One can be doing something else while the machine is beating away.

If your space or budget prevent your having a heavy-duty mixer, the small inexpensive hand-held electric beater is a wonderful help in creaming butter, beating in the sugar and eggs, as well as whipping up egg whites for meringues.

An electric mixer (hand-held or heavy-duty) is a necessity when adding a syrup/or melted chocolate to egg whites which must be beaten at the same time that the addition is being made.

Food Processor

The food processor is superb for grinding nuts. If the recipe calls for broken nuts or coarsely chopped nuts, use the shredding disk on your processor. If the recipe calls for ground nuts, use the steel chopping knife, processing with on/off bursts until the desired consistency is achieved. If a recipe calls for 3 cups of ground nuts, process 1 cup at a time for consistently uniform results. Watch that you don't end up with nut butter.

Except for whipping egg whites, which it cannot do, the food processor is a speedy demon at mixing cookie dough. It cannot make a huge batch of dough, which may be a limitation at times. Be careful not to overprocess after adding the flour. Run the machine just long enough barely to incorporate the flour.

Blender

The blender can also be used to grind nuts, but it will only do a small quantity at a time. Be careful, too, that the nuts don't gum up and form a mass. If that should happen, push them through a strainer to separate them again.

Measuring Equipment

Glass and clear plastic measuring cups should be used to measure liquid ingredients. Put the measuring pitcher at eye level for accuracy.

Measuring cups for dry ingredients (such as flour, sugar, nuts, etc.) are made of metal or plastic and usually come in sets of four, ranging in size from ¼ cup to 1 cup. When measuring, use the cup to scoop into the dry ingredient, overfilling it, and then level it off with a metal spatula or the straight side of a knife.

Measuring spoons also come in sets of four, from ¼ teaspoon to 1 tablespoon. Measurements should be accurate, with the tops leveled off with a spatula or knife. If a recipe call for ⅛ teaspoon, fill the ¼ teaspoon measure and remove half of it.

Nut Grinder

There are nut grinders available that clamp on the edge of a table or counter and grind nuts beautifully. They pose a problem in today's small kitchen. Apart from storage, the average kitchen today does not have a table or appropriate work counter to which something can be clamped. Both the food processor and the blender can grind nuts.

Nutmeg Grinder and Grater

Apart from the large number of cookie recipes that call for nutmeg, it is a spice that is used in many foods — i.e., cheese sauces, meat dishes, puddings and fruit desserts. For that reason I think a nutmeg grinder or grater is an essential kitchen tool. The flavor of freshly ground nutmeg is far superior to that of the packaged ground spice. I think the nutmeg grinder (similiar to a pepper mill) is much more convenient than the little nutmeg grater. The grater is small, with fine holes, and has a compartment at the top with a cover that lifts up; the compartment is used for storing the nutmeg between gratings. The grinder, on the other hand, holds the nutmeg inside it and does not require the cleaning that the grater does. I also feel the nutmeg is fresher tasting with a grinder.

Ovens

Ovens usually have 5 positions available for the 2 oven racks. Many of these recipes specify adjusting the rack to divide the oven into thirds. This simply means that the upper rack is in the slot below the uppermost one and the lower rack in the slot above the lowest one. This placement is done when you are baking two sheets of cookies at a time. About halfway through the baking time, or a little more than halfway, reverse the cookie sheets from the upper to the lower and turn them from front to back. When baking one sheet of cookies, use the upper rack and check the time. One sheet of cookies will bake faster than two.

Also check the accuracy of your oven thermostat with a separate oven thermometer. Different ovens can vary widely. Remember that it takes 10 to 15 minutes to preheat an oven. If an oven is on for a long period of time, the later batches of cookies will cook in a shorter time.

Pastry Bag

Some of these receipes call for a pastry bag. There have been many improvements in pastry bags in recent years. A plastic-lined cloth pastry bag is preferable to a plain cloth one, but a plastic or plasticized cloth one is more supple and manageable than any other. The plastic ones are very thin and flexible. Both are imported, and so far I have not found any made in this country. The plastic and plasticized cloth ones are available in some specialty kitchen shops and mail order houses (see Sources, p. 224). The pastry bags sometimes come with a set of metal tips. You can also purchase the metal tips separately.

When using a pastry bag you will have better control if the cookie sheet is at a lower height than the standard 36 inches of the work counter. Table height of about 29 inches is ideal. If you are pressed for work space you can put the cookie sheet in the kitchen sink, which is usually the right height.

To fill a pastry bag, first fit it with the appropriate metal tip. Place the pastry bag in a tall narrow jar or glass and fold the top down, outside the glass, to form a deep cuff, about 4 inches deep. With a spatula, quickly fill the pastry bag, *never* more than two-thirds full. Unfold the cuff and twist the top of the bag closed. Hold the bag at right angles to the baking sheet. Use one hand to keep the bag tightly closed and the other hand to guide the tip in forming the desired shapes.

A pastry bag can also be made from a triangle of parchment paper. These triangles can be purchased from baking supply stores and are formed into a cone shape. They are held together either by staples or by folding the tops over. After filling, the tip is cut with scissors to make an opening of the desired size.

Learning to use a pastry bag is really worthwhile. Practice with mashed potatoes and experiment with the different tips until you feel completely comfortable and sure using them.

Pastry Brush

It's a good idea to have 2 pastry brushes, one for wet glazes such as egg, milk or egg whites, and one for use with dry ingredients such as flour or sugar. Use a brush with real bristles rather than nylon ones. Look for these in art supply stores as well as in kitchen shops. I also have a white goose feather (available in specialty shops) and use it for applying egg glazes.

Pastry Cloths

A pastry cloth is used to prevent the dough sticking as it is rolled out. The cloth is rubbed with as much flour as it will absorb and refloured as necessary. The cloth should be washed after use because the shortening or butter from the cookie dough will stay on the cloth and become rancid. One can substitute wax paper for the cloth. The cloth, however, can be placed in the freezer, which will chill it somewhat — a help with delicate dough.

Pastry Wheel

Pastry wheels come with a plain edge (sometimes called a pizza cutter) or a crimped edge (sometimes known as a jagger). A dual one with a plain and a crimped cutter is available. The wheel is useful for dividing sheets of crackers, and the crimped wheel gives a nice professional-looking edge.

Rolling Pin

The longer and heavier the pin, the better it will work. There are long straight pins and thicker ones with ball bearings in the handles. I have both and like to use both, but some cooks will only use the one with the ball bearings and some will only use the straight one.

Rolling Pin Cover

The cover is meant to be used in conjunction with a pastry cloth, and like the cloth should be rubbed with flour before using. The cover should be washed after use. The standard covers are too short for the rolling pin, and I have not found them very satisfactory. They also leave their imprint on the dough. For that reason one must either keep the rolling pin well floured or (with certain doughs) use two sheets of wax paper.

Rulers

You will find a ruler a necessary tool for measuring the thickness of dough, for marking a rolled log of refrigerator cookies for slicing, or for marking off a cake into even squares or rectangles. It's also useful for checking the diameters of cookie cutters or size of pans.

Sifter

A sifter is used not only for sifting flour but also for sifting confectioners' (powdered) sugar and for sifting brown sugar. The lumps in sugar will not disappear in the baking. I think the 1-cup sifters that are sold are really too small to be practical and feel a 3-cup one is a better size.

A strainer can be used instead of a sifter. Strainers sometimes have a finer mesh than sifters. When using either a strainer or a sifter for flour or cornmeal, some particles may not pass through the screen. In that case, add them to the sifted flour.

Spatulas

Spatulas, both rubber and metal, are a necessity for general cooking as well as for cookie making. Rubber spatulas come in three sizes, the most useful being the small and the medium. I like to use the small size when making drop cookies to scrape dough from a spoon. The medium size is helpful for scraping dough out of a mixing bowl. The metal one is used for transferring baked cookies to the cooling rack and should be flexible and as wide as possible. I also have a narrow metal spatula which I use for leveling off dry ingredients when measuring them.

In addition to these I have a French wooden spatula which is about the size of a wooden spoon except that it is flat and has no bowl. I like this for creaming butter when I mix by hand.

Timer

For cookie baking where a few minutes can mean disaster, a timer is essential. Set it for a shorter time than is called for and check on the cookies, rather than assuming that the time given in a recipe will apply to your oven.

Working with Ingredients

Almonds

To blanch shelled almonds, cover them with boiling water and let them stand for 5 minutes. Drain the almonds and pour cold water over them. The skins will slip off easily.

To cut or shred blanched almonds, do it while they are still moist and warm.

If almonds are not to be used immediately, store them in a covered jar in the refrigerator or freezer.

Almond Paste

If you buy almond paste in a foil package, squeeze it gently to make sure it's still fresh. If it has completely hardened, it's too dry. Almond paste in cans seems to stay fresher. Domestic almond paste is usually sweeter than the imported. Some specialty shops, or perhaps a friendly bakery shop, sell almond paste in bulk (see Sources, p. 224).

If you have a food processor you can make your own almond paste (see p. 5), but it will not be quite as smooth as the purchased variety.

True almond paste consists of ground almonds and sugar (usually sugar syrup) which is passed through heavy rollers. A mixture such as that is much too heavy and stiff for any home equipment. A satisfactory substitute can be made as follows:

4 ounces of blanched almonds   ¼ teaspoon almond extract
½ cup powdered sugar   1 egg white

In the work bowl fitted with the steel knife, grind the almonds until fine. Freeze the almonds first for more satisfactory results. Add the sugar, almond extract, and egg white. Process until smooth. This mixture can be kept in the refrigerator in an airtight container for several weeks.

Baking Powder

The baking powder used in these recipes is double-acting baking powder. This means that the leavening action of the baking powder starts to work when it is added to the ingredients and is *reactivated* by the heat of the oven. Single-action baking powder acts only once — when it is added to the ingredients — so it is not suitable for many cookie doughs which have to rest, or to be chilled, before baking.

If you suddenly discover that your larder has run out of baking powder, you can substitute for each teaspoon of baking powder ½ teaspoon cream of tartar and ¼ teaspoon baking soda.

Butter

All the recipes in this book call for unsalted butter and some specify clarified butter.

To clarify butter: Cut the butter into pieces and place them in a heavy saucepan over moderate heat. When the butter has completely melted, skim the foam off the surface and strain the clear yellow liquid into a bowl, leaving the milky residue in the bottom of the pan.

Clarified butter keeps in the refrigerator for weeks. It is used in general cooking for sautéing and for some sauce making because it burns much less readily than ordinary butter. (The milky residue in the bottom of the pan can be stirred into soups and sauces as an enrichment.)

Chocolate

Chocolate is made from the fruit of the cocoa tree, which is grown in the moist tropical climates of the world. The fruit is in the form of pods and the cocoa beans are contained in these pods, 20 to 25 beans in a pod. The pods are harvested and the beans removed. The beans are fermented for some days and then dried. It is the dried beans that are shipped to cocoa and chocolate factories for processing.

The beans are blended by the chocolate manufacturer according to a formula which may be unique to each manufacturer. The beans are then roasted, which loosens the outer shells. After roasting they are processed to remove the loosened outer shell and break the bean into bits known as "nibs."

The nibs contain about 53 percent cocoa butter and are the basis for all chocolate and cocoa products. The nibs are ground, which liquefies the cocoa butter, and the resulting substance is called chocolate "liquor."

Unsweetened Baking Chocolate

The chocolate liquor is poured into molds, cooled, and hardened. The result is the purest chocolate available.

Semisweet Chocolate

Semisweet chocolate is made from the chocolate liquor with the addition of cocoa butter and sugar. It contains about 35 percent chocolate liquor.

Sweet Chocolate

Sweet chocolate is usually in the form of candy bars or chips or coatings on candies and is made from about 15 percent chocolate liquor with the addition of sugar, cocoa butter, and flavorings.

Cocoa

Cocoa is made by pressing most of the cocoa butter out of the chocolate liquor. The hard brown cake that remains is cooled, pulverized, and sifted to produce cocoa.

Premelted Chocolate

This is made from cocoa, hydrogenated cottonseed oil, partly hydrogenated soybean oil, coconut oil, and preservatives. I don't feel that it is a satisfactory substitute for the flavor of unsweetened or semisweet chocolate.

Chocolate Bits or Morsels

Since these are meant to retain their shape when baked in cookies, etc., they have a higher viscosity than regular chocolate. They average 29 percent chocolate and 29 percent cocoa butter. Although they can be substituted for semisweet chocolate, I don't like the flavor and texture as well. When melted, their texture seems different from regular melted chocolate. For that reason the only time I use them in melted form is to spread them on warm bar cookies as an icing.

Chocolate Substitutions

For 1 ounce of unsweetened chocolate, combine 3 tablespoons of unsweetened cocoa with 1 tablespoon of unsalted butter, shortening, or cocoa butter.

For 1 ounce of semisweet chocolate, add 3 tablespoons granulated sugar to the above cocoa-and-butter blend.

To make unsweetened chocolate into semisweet chocolate, combine and melt together 1 ounce unsweetened chocolate, 3½ tablespoons granulated sugar, and 1 tablespoon unsalted butter, shortening, or cocoa butter. This will make 3 ounces semisweet chocolate.

Melting Chocolate with Other Ingredients

When melting chocolate with other ingredients, such as coffee, liqueur, or butter, place the liquid in the pan first and then add the chocolate to it. When combining it with butter, such as in brownies, melt the butter before adding the chocolate.

Melting Chocolate by Itself

Unsweetened and semisweet chocolate should be melted in the top of a double boiler set over hot water or melted in a small pan that is set in a larger pan containing a small amount of hot water. Chocolate can also be melted by placing the pan containing the chocolate in a low oven (not over 110°F.) for an hour or so. It can also be melted by placing the pan in a moderate oven for about 5 minutes.

It is important that the temperature of the chocolate not exceed 110°F. or it will burn.

Be sure that the pan in which you place the chocolate is absolutely dry and never stir chocolate with a wet spoon! The introduction of even this small amount of liquid into the melting chocolate causes the chocolate to become rough and lumpy. If the chocolate does become lumpy, stir in 1 to 2 tablespoons of homogenized vegetable shortening for each 6 ounces of chocolate. It won't affect the flavor but it will smooth out the chocolate.

Cocoa

The cocoa called for in these recipes is unsweetened cocoa powder. The better it is, the better the cookie or brownie. I use imported Dutch cocoa.

Eggs

Extra-large eggs were used in all of these recipes.

Egg whites that are to be beaten for meringues, etc., should be at room temperature to achieve proper volume. If they are cold, place them in a bowl and set the bowl in warm water. Also, they are affected by humidity. Eggs do not mount as well in damp weather and their volume and stability are affected. Therefore, making meringues on a wet or humid day can be discouraging.

Egg whites can be frozen; they can be thawed and refrozen safely. One egg white measures 2 tablespoons. Rather than store frozen egg whites in a jar, I freeze them in small plastic containers of individual ice-cube size. When they are frozen, I pop them out of the containers and store the frozen cubes in a plastic bag in the freezer. They will defrost overnight in the refrigerator or in about 2 hours at room temperature. Defrosting can be hastened by placing the egg whites in a bowl and setting the bowl in a larger bowl containing hot water, changing the water periodically to keep it hot.

Egg Yolks

Egg yolks are used both raw and cooked in baking. *To hard-cook them,* follow this procedure: Separate the eggs, being careful not to break the yolks. Reserve or freeze the whites. Place the yolks in a custard cup or small bowl (I use a small stainless-steel bowl). Set the cup or bowl in a saucepan. Bring water to a boil in a separate kettle and slowly pour the boiling water around the bowl containing the yolks. Continue pouring the water until the bowl is submerged and filled with water. Place the saucepan over moderate heat; keeping the water at a simmer, cook the yolks for 15 minutes. Do not let the water boil. Remove the yolks from the water and pat them dry on paper towels before using.

Usually hard-cooked eggs are pressed through a sieve into the bowl of other ingredients.

Raw egg yolks can be frozen, but they do not soften completely when thawed. Hard-cooked yolks can be frozen successfully. To freeze them, cool them, then wrap individually in plastic; make sure the wrapping is airtight. Freeze. Let them thaw wrapped; then push through a sieve to use.

Here is an even better way: Purée a hard-cooked egg yolk with 1 tablespoon unsalted butter and freeze the mixture. Do no more than 2 egg yolks and 2 tablespoons of butter per package. When thawed, the purée can be creamed right along with the butter before adding sugar and other eggs. Be sure to reduce the amount of butter called for in the recipe by the amount of butter that has been puréed with the frozen yolk or yolks.

Important: Thaw frozen egg yolks in the refrigerator. If you are pressed for time and want to thaw them at room temperature, use them as soon as thawed. *Never* let egg yolks sit at room temperature for any length of time as they can easily breed bacteria. Frozen yolks will thaw overnight in the refrigerator, or they can be thawed at room temperature in 1 to 2 hours.

Extracts

When buying extracts, make sure the label reads "pure extract" of vanilla, lemon, etc. Don't use imitation flavors. Since extracts contain a large proportion of alcohol, keep them tightly closed to prevent evaporation.

You can make your own *vanilla extract* by placing vanilla beans in brandy (an inexpensive brandy is fine) and letting them steep for about 2 weeks. Leave the beans in the jar or bottle and reuse them for 2 more batches. Use about 6 beans to 1 cup (8 oz.) brandy. All the recipes in this book call for regular vanilla extract. The brandy vanilla extract is quite strong and should be approached with caution. You'll have to experiment to suit your own taste.

Filberts or Hazelnuts

To *blanch* these, place shelled nuts in a 350°F. oven for 10 to 15 minutes, or until the brown skin is dark in color. When nuts are cool enough to handle, rub them in a towel or between your hands to flake off the brown skin.

Flour

Flour is milled from hard wheat and soft wheat; hard wheat flour has a higher gluten content. Gluten is an important protein, found in wheat flours. Flour with a high gluten content is preferred for bread making, while lower gluten content is preferred for cakes, cookies, and pastry. Unless otherwise specified, all of the recipes in this book call for all-purpose flour. This is bleached flour. The gluten content of unbleached flour is higher than that of bleached flour; although it is great for breads, it is not recommended for cookies.

A few recipes call for cake flour, which should be plain cake flour, *not* self-rising.

Although it may be labeled presifted, flour does pack down, and this can affect the success of a recipe. Flour should be sifted before being measured and then resifted with the other dry ingredients. Use a metal or plastic measuring cup to scoop into the flour, fill to overflowing, and level it with a metal spatula or straight edge of a knife. Never pack it down. Sift it onto a piece of wax paper and place the sifter on a second piece of wax paper. Measure the necessary amount from the first piece of wax paper, put it into the sifter, add the other dry ingredients, and sift all together.

All-Purpose Flour

All-purpose flour is made from a mixture of hard and soft wheat.

Cake Flour

Cake flour comes in two forms: self-rising, which contains a leavening agent such as baking powder, and regular cake flour, which contains no leavening agent. It is made from soft wheat and is low in gluten.

Unbleached Flour

Unbleached flour is bleached by aging rather than chemicals. It contains more hard wheat than all-purpose flour and has a higher gluten content. It is preferred for bread making.

Whole-Wheat Flour

Whole-wheat flour contains the whole germ of the wheat. Because of its higher fat content it should be kept in the refrigerator or freezer if it is to be stored for any length of time.

Whole-Wheat Pastry Flour

This is mostly available in health-food stores. It is made from soft wheat and is suitable for pastry and crackers.

Rye Flour

Rye flour is lower in gluten content than wheat flour and is usually combined with wheat flour in bread making.

Soy Flour

Soy flour is very high in protein and adds valuable nutrition to foods that include it as an ingredient. Processed from soybeans, soy flour comes in different forms:

Full-fat flour contains over 35 percent protein and about 20 percent fat.
Low-fat flour contains almost 45 percent protein and about 6 percent fat.
Defatted flour contains about 50 percent protein and less than 1 percent fat.

Defatted soy flour comes in flake form and in granulated form. The flake form does not sift. Most of the granulated soy flour does sift, but not all. There are no trade standards of extraction, mill size, or screen size, so there are wide variations in soy flours.

If you cannot sift soy flour, stir it before spooning it into a measuring cup and leveling it.

All the soy flour used in the recipes was defatted soy flour in a granulated form which was sifted.

One further note: some old cookbooks direct the cook to add the soy flour to the shortening rather than to the other flour. The varieties of soybeans have changed since the 1930s and that direction is no longer applicable.

Since soy flour contains no gluten, it can be used only in limited quantities in baking since gluten is an essential part of the baking process.

Soy flour can be substituted in many cookie recipes in the following proportions: From each cup of flour, remove 3 tablespoons of flour and substitute 3 tablespoons of soy flour. This flour is available at most health-food stores.

I would not recommend using soy flour in delicately flavored cookies. Limit its use to those cookies that contain a fair amount of spices or ingredients with a strong flavor such as raisins and other fruits, chocolate, peanut butter, etc.

Fruits

Dried fruits and candied fruits are difficult to chop. The easiest way to proceed is to cut them with scissors.

Raisins and currants should be soft for cookie baking. *To plump them,* place them in a steamer and steam over boiling water for about 5 minutes. Or boil them for a few minutes. Drain them and dry between paper towels.

Nuts

Nuts in cans will be fresher than those in bags. If you buy them loose, make sure they are fresh. They should be stored in the refrigerator or, preferably, the freezer.

Peanuts and other nuts can be chopped in a food processor or blender. Lacking one, place the nuts in a tea towel or between sheets of wax paper and hit them with a mallet or the flat side of a cleaver, or use a rolling pin. If frozen, nuts become brittle and break more easily.

See also information on Almonds, Filberts, Walnuts.

Oats

The kind of oats called for in these recipes is either Old Fashioned (cooks in 5 minutes) or Quick Oats (cooks in 1 minute). Instant oatmeal is not as satisfactory and should not be used. My preference is for the Old Fashioned.

Rosewater

Rosewater was a common ingredient in many old recipes. It is also used in many desserts in India and the Near East. It can be purchased at some drugstores and is available at specialty food shops (see Sources, p. 224).

Seeds

Caraway seeds, cumin seeds, sesame seeds, poppy seeds, and aniseeds, like nuts, contain oils which can easily become stale. These too should be stored in the refrigerator or freezer.

The best way I have found to sprinkle sesame or other seeds is to place a round piece of foil in a funnel and poke a very small hole in it. Place the seeds in the funnel and tap or gently shake. The seeds will come out in a nice even flow with no waste. Lacking a funnel, make a cone out of foil.

Soybeans

Although only one or two of these recipes specifically call for soybeans, they can be added to many others, either in place of or in addition to nuts. Toasted soybeans, available at health-food stores, should be coarsely chopped for use in cookies. They are a good source of protein and increase the nutritive value of many foods.

Spices

Buy the best-quality spices you can find and buy in small quantities. Refrigerator storage would be ideal but we all have space problems, so buying small quantities will help. Store spices away from heat and light, if possible, as both cause loss of flavor.

Sugars

Sugar, primarily made from sugar cane, is refined from the juice or sugar liquor, as it is called in the trade. Granulated sugar is the purest of the sugars and contains over 99 percent sucrose. It is removed from the sugar liquor and crystallized. Dark brown or light brown sugars are removed from the liquor stream and crystallized. Their grains are of varying sizes and contain more moisture than granulated or brownulated sugar. Brownulated sugar, which is higher in sucrose than brown sugar, is processed into even grains to allow it to pour more easily. Most cooks do not consider it a substitute for brown sugar. Confectioners' sugar and powdered sugar are the same thing. They are sugars which have been milled to be very fine and have a small percentage of cornstarch added to absorb moisture. After the extraction of the brown sugars from the liquor stream, the residue is blackstrap molasses. It is not processed to be edible in this country and is used in cattle feed.

The *granulated sugar* called for in these recipes is regular granulated cane sugar, not superfine or quick-dissolving.

The *brown sugar* called for, whether it is light brown or old-fashioned dark brown, is not "brownulated." Brown sugar should be sifted to remove lumps. Unlike flour, brown sugar to be measured should be *firmly* packed down in the cup until it is level.

Confectioners' sugar should be sifted to remove the lumps. Once it is sifted it seems to stay lump free, so it is a good idea to sift the whole box when you open it.

To sprinkle powdered sugar, use a small strainer and tap the handle to shake the sugar evenly on the cookies.

Crystal or pearl sugar is a coarse sugar that is available at specialty shops (see Sources, p. 224). A substitute can be made by crushing lump sugar. This is used for sprinkling on tops of cookies for a decorative touch.

Fruit Sugar or Fructose: There has been a good deal written lately about this sugar. It has become something of a fad now that it is available in pure form. Usually found in health-food stores, it is quite expensive. Although it contains the same number of calories as granulated sugar (sucrose), it is much sweeter, so lesser quantities of it will be needed. If you wish to use fructose, the approximate equivalents in sweetening ability are as follows:

2/3 cup granulated fructose equals 1 cup granulated cane sugar
½ cup fructose equals ¾ cup granulated cane sugar
1/3 cup fructose equals ½ cup granulated cane sugar

There is one distinct advantage to fructose: It does not need insulin to get into the liver and body cells, so there is no sudden demand on the body for insulin; this is important for diabetics. Fructose is also useful for those people who have hypoglycemia and tend to overproduce insulin when ingesting sucrose.

Cooked Sugar: Sugar syrup is made by combining water and sugar over moderate heat. Dissolve the sugar slowly and stir constantly until you can see that the sugar is dissolved. If all the sugar is not dissolved, the entire batch can crystallize when cooled. To prevent this, continue to wash down the sides of the pan with a brush dipped in cold water. An alternate way is to cover the pan with a tight-fitting lid. The resulting condensation of steam will wash down the sides of the pan. After the sugar has dissolved, the syrup is boiled to evaporate the water and thicken the syrup. A candy thermometer is the most accurate way to determine temperatures. Lacking a thermometer, the temperature can be judged as follows:

Thread stage: 230 to 234°F. The syrup will form a thin thread and hang from the end of a wooden spoon.

Soft ball: 234 to 240°F. A bit of slightly cooled syrup dropped in a cup of very cold water will form a soft ball.

Firm ball: 244 to 248°F. Syrup dropped into very cold water forms a ball which retains its shape when removed from the water.

Hard ball: 250 to 266°F. Syrup dropped into very cold water forms a ball which retains its shape when removed from the water but can be flattened if pressed.

Soft crack: 270 to 290°F. Syrup dropped into very cold water separates into bits which are hard but not brittle.

Hard crack: 300 to 310°F. Syrup dropped into very cold water separates into bits which are hard and brittle.

Caramelized: 320°F. Syrup turns brown.

Flavored Sugars

Vanilla sugar is often referred to in cookbooks. To make it yourself, bury 2 or 3 vanilla beans in a pound of sugar in an airtight container. Let the mixture stand about 1 week before using. Replenish sugar as used, and add a fresh bean after 4 months. Vanilla sugar is used more for the aroma than for the taste; it is not usually a substitute for vanilla extract. If you wish to use it as a substitute for the extract, allow 1 tablespoon of vanilla sugar for each ¼ teaspoon vanilla extract and decrease the quantity of unflavored sugar accordingly. For example, if a recipe calls for 1 cup of sugar and 1 teaspoon vanilla extract, you would use 4 tablespoons vanilla sugar and ¾ cup sugar.

    Cinnamon sugar: Mix together 2 cups granulated sugar and 2 tablespoons ground cinnamon. Store in a covered jar.

    Lemon sugar: Grate the rind of 6 lemons or pare the rind, cutting a very thin layer. Peel only the yellow skin or rind, not the white pith underneath, which is very bitter. Grind the lemon rind very fine in a food processor or blender. Measure the grated or ground rind and add twice as much sugar (about 1 cup). Mash the sugar and lemon together. The sugar should be very slightly damp. If it looks very dry, add 1 or 2 drops of lemon juice. Keep in a covered jar in the refrigerator. Use 1 tablespoon lemon sugar as substitute for 1 teaspoon grated lemon rind.

Orange sugar: Follow the same recipe as for lemon sugar, subsituting 4 oranges for 6 lemons.

Syrups

To measure honey, molasses, or other syrups, butter a measuring cup inside and out and *pour* the honey or molasses into the cup. The butter keeps the honey from sticking to the cup.

Walnuts

To blanch shelled walnuts, follow the same procedure that is used for almonds (see p. 13). When nuts are cool enough to handle, rub the skins off between your hands or in a towel.

Drop Cookies

Drop cookies are formed by filling a teaspoon or tablespoon with dough. Using a small rubber spatula or the back of a second spoon, push the dough onto the cookie sheet.

Most cookie dough described as being for drop cookies can be formed into rolls and chilled and sliced into rounds. Most cookie dough intended to be formed into rolls and chilled can be used unchilled to make drop cookies.

Chilling Cookie Dough

With the exception of dough intended for drop cookies, most cookie dough is easier to handle if it is chilled until it is firm but not hard before being formed. If a buttery dough is too cold and hard, it can crack and will be very difficult to roll. The dough should not stick to your fingers but should "give" slightly when pressed. If the dough is unusually soft and sticky, chill the pastry cloth, rolling pin, and, if possible, the board.

Refrigerator Cookies

To form a round or oval, place the mixed dough on a long sheet of wax paper, spreading it lengthwise. Fold up the sides of the paper and press it against the dough, shaping it into a cylinder. If it is too soft, chill it until it will hold the shape you want. When formed into a log, wrap it in more wax paper or foil and place it on a cookie sheet or other flat surface. Freeze or chill the log for several hours or overnight. It can then be sliced into rounds. The log can also be formed into an oval, rather than a round, by flattening it slightly.

To form a square, line a box (such as a foil, plastic wrap, or wax-paper box) with wax paper, fill it with dough, and freeze it or chill it until firm.

To form a crescent-shaped log, the dough must not be too firm. Wrap the dough in wax paper and form an oval log. Place the log on top of a rolling pin. With your hands, gently mold the outside edges of the oval partway around the rolling pin so that the edges are thinner than the center and curve around the rolling pin. Wrap the log in wax paper or foil and chill for several hours or overnight before slicing. If the dough is frozen, let it thaw slightly before slicing.

Rolling Out Cookie Dough

Roll out the dough on a floured pastry cloth with a floured rolling pin, or roll dough between 2 sheets of wax paper. Use as little flour as possible for this step, since too much flour can toughen the cookies. Many people prefer using wax paper for this reason.

Rolling dough between sheets of wax paper is particularly good for very soft doughs that are high in butter content, or for cookies that have to be rolled paper thin. Roll the dough out, peel off the top sheet of paper, and invert the paper (used side down) on your work surface. Turn the dough onto this sheet and peel off and reverse the top sheet. Continue to roll, reversing the paper. If necessary replace with fresh paper. If dough starts to soften, return it, in the wax paper, to the refrigerator. A brief chilling will firm the dough and the paper will peel off. When the dough reaches the desired thickness, remove the top sheet. Cut out the cookies with the bottom sheet of paper in place. Chill the cookies on the paper until they are firm enough to transfer to the baking sheet.

Roll only a small amount of dough at a time and keep the rest refrigerated.

Another way is to roll out the dough directly on a buttered and floured flat cookie sheet. Cut out the shapes right on the sheet, removing the surplus from between them.

Cutting Out Cookies

When dough has been rolled out to desired thickness, cut out shapes, plain or fancy, with cookie cutters.

Use flour on cookie cutters only if the cutter sticks and the dough is soft and sticky. Be sparing with flour. Sift a little into a shallow dish. Dip the cutter into the flour, and shake off the excess.

Keep shapes simple when cutting soft dough.

Since cut cookies do not spread much in baking, they can usually be placed 1 inch apart on the baking sheet.

Bars and Squares

Batter for these is usually spread out and smoothed with a flexible spatula, but it can be done by hand. Keep running palms over an ice cube to keep them cool and wet, which will prevent sticking. Pat the batter level, making sure it fills in the corners.

Cooling and Storing Cookies

Unless otherwise specified, remove cookies from the baking sheet or foil and cool them on a wire rack.

When cookies are completely cooled, store them in an airtight container. Store crisp ones separately from soft ones; the latter can be kept moist by placing half an apple in the container.

Freezing Cookies and Dough

Baked cookies are best eaten when fresh. Freezing them very often affects the taste. You can, however, freeze many of them in unbaked form and store them for 2 or 3 months. Those that are most successfully frozen in unbaked form are plain cookies, nothing with candied fruit, for example.

Drop cookie dough can be formed into a log and frozen for slicing. The dough can also be formed into small balls and frozen. Cut-out cookies can also be frozen. To freeze balls or cut-outs, spread them out on wax paper on a cookie sheet or other flat pan and place them in the freezer. When completely frozen, peel the shapes off the wax paper and store them in an airtight container.

Drop Cookies

Almond Tacos

While they are still warm, these are folded in half like a taco and become crisp as they cool.

2½ ounces blanched almonds
¼ pound (1 stick) unsalted butter
½ cup granulated sugar

3 Tablespoons all-purpose flour
2 Tablespoons cream

Grind the almonds very fine in a food processor or blender. Cream the butter with the sugar until light and fluffy. Sift the flour into the butter and sugar, beating it in thoroughly. Add almonds and cream. Chill for at least 1 hour.

Preheat oven to 375°F., and adjust the rack to divide the oven into thirds. Line 2 cookie sheets with foil, or butter them lightly. Using a spoon and a rubber spatula, or 2 spoons, place teaspoons of the dough 4 inches apart on the prepared cookie sheets. Bake for about 10 minutes. About halfway through the baking time, reverse the cookie sheets from the upper to the lower rack and turn them from front to back. Cookies are done when they are nicely and evenly browned. Leaving the oven door ajar, remove one sheet at a time from the oven. After the cookies have cooled for 1 minute, scoop them up with a flexible spatula, fold them in half, and transfer them to a rack to cool.

YIELD: 36 cookies

Oatmeal Lace Wafers

An old-fashioned classic with a well-deserved reputation.

¼ cup sifted all-purpose flour
½ teaspoon ground allspice
½ teaspoon ground cinnamon
½ teaspoon ground cloves
½ teaspoon ground ginger
½ teaspoon salt
¼ teaspoon baking powder
¼ pound (1 stick) unsalted butter

1/3 cup granulated sugar
1/3 cup firmly packed dark or
   light brown sugar
1 egg
1 teaspoon vanilla extract
1 cup old-fashioned rolled oats
1/3 cup chopped walnuts

Preheat oven to 350°F., and adjust the racks to divide the oven into thirds. Butter 2 cookie sheets, or line them with foil. Sift the flour before measuring and resift it with the spices, salt and baking powder. Cream the butter with both sugars until light. Add the egg and the vanilla, beating them in well. Add the oats and the sifted dry ingredients. Lastly fold in chopped walnuts. Using a spoon and a rubber spatula, or 2 spoons, place lightly rounded teaspoons of the batter about 3 inches apart on the prepared sheets. Flatten mounds with tines of a fork that has been dipped into cold water.

Bake for 10 to 12 minutes. About halfway through the baking time, reverse the cookie sheets from the upper to the lower racks and turn them from front to back. Transfer to a rack to cool.

YIELD: 40 to 45 wafers
VARIATION: Add ¼ cup raisins and reduce walnuts to ¼ cup.

Pignoli Cookies

For those who like the distinctive taste of pignoli *(pine nuts), another recipe that uses them is V's Favorite Pine-Nut Cookies, p. 137.*

1 cup sifted all-purpose flour
¼ pound (1 stick) unsalted butter
½ cup granulated sugar

1 egg yolk
1 teaspoon vanilla extract
½ cup pine nuts

Preheat oven to 300°F., and adjust the racks to divide the oven into thirds. Butter and flour a baking sheet; shake off excess flour. Sift the flour before measuring it. Cream the butter until light. Gradually beat in the sugar. Beat in the egg yolk and vanilla. Add the sifted flour, blending in until flour is just incorporated. Fold in the pine nuts. Using a spoon and a rubber spatula, or 2 spoons, put teaspoons of the dough about 2 inches apart on the cookie sheets.

Bake the cookies for 20 to 25 minutes, or until they have turned pale gold. After about 14 minutes, reverse the baking sheets from the upper to the lower racks and turn them from front to back. Transfer to a rack to cool.

YIELD: 30 cookies

Stove-Top Cocoa Oatmeal Cookies

These are fast and easy. Children enjoy making them as well as eating them.

½ cup milk
¼ pound (1 stick) unsalted butter,
   cut into pieces
6 Tablespoons unsweetened cocoa
   powder

1 2/3 cups granulated sugar
1 teaspoon vanilla extract
½ cup peanut butter
3 cups rolled oats, preferably old-
   fashioned

Put the milk and butter in a heavy saucepan over medium heat. Add cocoa and sugar and stir them in well. Bring the mixture to a boil and let it boil for 1 minute. Remove the pan from the heat. Beat in the vanilla, peanut butter and the rolled oats, blending well. Using a spoon and a rubber spatula, or 2 spoons, place teaspoons of the mixture on sheets of wax paper to cool and set.

YIELD: 48 cookies
VARIATIONS: Omit the peanut butter and use ½ cup shredded coconut or finely chopped pecans or walnuts.

Apple Whole-Wheat Drops
These are full of goodness, with raw apples, raisins and nuts and soy flour.

2 cups sifted all-purpose flour
¼ cup sifted whole-wheat pastry flour
¼ cup unsifted soy flour
½ teaspoon baking powder
½ teaspoon baking soda
½ teaspoon salt
1 teaspoon ground cinnamon
½ teaspoon ground nutmeg
¼ teaspoon ground cloves
¼ teaspoon ground allspice

¼ pound (1 stick) unsalted butter
1¼ cups firmly packed dark brown sugar
2 eggs
¼ cup milk or apple juice or orange juice
1¼ cups chopped unpeeled raw apple
1 cup raisins
¾ to 1 cup chopped shelled walnuts, cashews, pecans or hazelnuts

Preheat oven to 375°F., and adjust the racks to divide the oven into thirds. Butter 2 cookie sheets, or line them with foil. Sift the white and whole-wheat flours before measuring and resift them with the soy flour, baking powder, baking soda, salt and all the spices. Cream the butter until soft. Beat in the sugar until light and fluffy. Add the eggs, one at a time, beating after each addition. Add the sifted dry ingredients alternately with the milk or juice. Stir in the apples, raisins and nuts.

Using a spoon and a rubber spatula, or 2 spoons, place rounded teaspoons of the dough about 1½ inches apart on the cookie sheets. Bake for 10 to 12 minutes, or until light brown. After about 7 minutes, reverse the cookie sheets from the upper to the lower rack and turn them from front to back. Transfer to a rack to cool.

YIELD: 48 cookies

Tuiles (Almond Tiles)

A delectable French cookie which takes its name from its shape; these are curved like old-fashioned roof tiles. Speed is of the essence in forming them so, although you can prepare more than one baking sheet, it is advisable to bake only one batch at a time. The rounded shape of the cookies is formed by placing them face up on a rolling pin, straight-sided bottle, inverted large ring mold, long thick wooden dowel, or anything else round you can think of. They become crisp very quickly so you have to work fast while they are hot, shaping them one at a time.

2 ounces (½ stick) softened unsalted butter
½ cup granulated sugar
2 egg whites (¼ cup)
5 Tablespoons *unsifted* cake flour
1/3 cup finely ground almonds

½ teaspoon vanilla extract
¼ teaspoon almond extract
 (optional)
½ cup blanched almonds, sliced or
 slivered

Preheat oven to 425°F., and place a rack at the middle level. Thoroughly butter 2 baking sheets and set them aside. Cream the softened butter with the sugar and beat until soft and fluffy. Add the egg whites, beating for just a few seconds to blend them in. Sift the flour over the batter and fold it in with a rubber spatula. Fold in the *ground* almonds and the extracts. Using a spoon and a rubber spatula, scoop up ½ teaspoons of the batter and scrape them onto the baking sheet, placing the mounds 3 inches apart. With the dampened back of a spoon, spread the batter out to a diameter of about 2½ inches; it will be very thin. Top each one with a sprinkling of the *sliced* or *slivered* almonds.

Bake until the edges are slightly browned; it may only take 4 or 5 minutes, depending on the thickness of the cookie. When the cookies are done, remove the baking sheet from the oven and rest it on the open oven door, if possible; this will keep the cookies warm. Quickly lift one cookie off the sheet with a flexible spatula and place it face up on the rounded surface. As the first ones harden into shape, remove them to make room for the later ones. Continue working fast, removing and forming the remaining cookies. If they have cooled too much to shape, return them to the oven for a few seconds to soften them.

Close the oven door and allow a few minutes for the temperature to return to 425°F. Continue baking and shaping the remainder of the cookies. Store them airtight.

YIELD: between 30 and 45 tiles, depending on the size of the mound of batter.

VARIATIONS:
1. Eliminate the finely ground almonds, add the grated rind of ½ orange, and blend in the sliced or slivered almonds instead of sprinkling them on top.
2. Substitute 1 cup chopped walnuts, reduce the flour to ¼ cup, and add 2 Tablespoons cream and 1 Tablespoon liqueur or rum.
3. Reduce the flour to 3 Tablespoons. Use 1 cup finely chopped (rice-size pieces) almonds and 1 whole egg. Increase vanilla to 1 teaspoon. Bake at 375°F. for 8 to 10 minutes. Cookies are formed from 1½ teaspoons of batter and flattened with the tines of a fork.

Arrowroot Wafers

This old-fashioned cookie is very plain and consequently nice and soothing. Arrowroot, being easily digested, used to be recommended for use in puddings or cookies for invalids and children. This recipe is from the redoubtable Mrs. Beeton, who was only 24 years old when she completed that fantastic Book of Household Management.

1 cup sifted all-purpose flour
½ cup arrowroot (see Note)
¼ pound (1 stick) unsalted butter
½ cup granulated sugar
3 eggs, well beaten

Preheat oven to 325°F., and adjust the racks to divide the oven into thirds. Butter 2 cookie sheets, or line them with foil. Sift the flour before measuring and resift it with the arrowroot. Cream the butter until soft. Beat in the sugar until light and fluffy. Add the beaten eggs (the mixture will look curdled), and stir in the flour and arrowroot. Using a teaspoon and a rubber spatula, or the back of a second spoon, place slightly rounded teaspoons of the dough about 1½ inches apart on the prepared cookie sheets. Flatten the mounds lightly with the back of a spoon that has been dipped into cold water.

Bake for 10 to 12 minutes, or until cookies are very lightly colored. The centers will still feel faintly soft and the edges will be lightly browned. After 6 or 7 minutes, reverse the sheets from the upper to the lower rack and turn them from front to back. Transfer to a rack to cool.

YIELD: 48 wafers

VARIATIONS: The dough, which is very soft, can be chilled until it is firm enough to form a log about 2 inches in diameter. Then freeze the log. While still frozen, slice it crosswise into rounds ⅛ inch thick. If you want to roll out the dough and cut it into shapes, work with about one third of the dough at a time. Since it is sticky dough to work with, you will have to use a well-floured pastry cloth and well-floured rolling pin. Also, keep turning the dough over so that both sides are floured.

NOTE: Arrowroot is the dried and powdered root of a plant that is found in Bermuda, the West Indian island of St. Vincent's, and other places. It is a starch that can substitute for flour as a thickening agent in cooking; 1 Tablespoon arrowroot equals 2½ Tablespoons flour in thickening ability. Most grocers sell it in small jars of 3⅛ ounces which equals ½ cup. However, I buy it in a larger quantity in health-food stores, and store it in a glass jar.

Banana Spice Drops

These are thick and soft, with the mingled flavors of bananas and spices.

2¼ cups sifted all-purpose flour
1½ teaspoons baking powder
½ teaspoon baking soda
½ teaspoon salt
1 teaspoon ground cinnamon
½ teaspoon ground ginger
¼ teaspoon ground nutmeg
6½ ounces (1 1/3 sticks) unsalted butter

2/3 cup firmly packed brown sugar
2 eggs
2 large or 3 medium-size ripe bananas, mashed (1 cup)
¾ cup raisins
¾ cup chopped nuts
½ teaspoon vanilla extract, *or* 2 teaspoons grated lemon rind

Preheat oven to 375°F., and adjust the racks to divide the oven into thirds. Sift the flour before measuring and resift it with the baking powder, baking soda, salt and spices. In a large mixing bowl, cream the butter. Beat in the sugar until light. Add the eggs one at a time, beating well after each addition. Add mashed banana and beat until well mixed. Transfer a heaping tablespoon of the flour mixture to a small bowl with the raisins and nuts, and toss to separate them and coat them lightly with the flour. Gradually add the sifted dry ingredients to the mixing bowl, beating until just incorporated. Stir in vanilla extract or lemon rind, and finally the floured raisins and nuts. Using a spoon and a rubber spatula, or 2 spoons, place heaping teaspoons of the dough about 2 inches apart on an unbuttered or foil-lined cookie sheet. Do not flatten the mounds of dough.

Bake the cookies for 14 to 18 minutes, or until they are lightly browned and spring back when gently pressed with a fingertip. Transfer them to a rack to cool.

YIELD: 48 cookies

Carrot Lemon Drops

The carrots help keep these delicious cookies soft and moist.

2 cups sifted all-purpose flour, *or*
  1½ cups sifted all-purpose flour
  and ½ cup sifted whole-wheat
  pastry flour
2 teaspoons baking powder
¼ teaspoon baking soda
¼ teaspoon salt
½ teaspoon ground cinnamon
¼ teaspoon ground nutmeg
¼ pound (1 stick) unsalted butter

½ cup firmly packed dark brown
  sugar
½ cup granulated sugar
1 egg
1 cup coarsely grated or shredded
  raw carrots
½ teaspoon vanilla extract
½ teaspoon lemon extract
2 teaspoons lemon rind
1 cup chopped nuts

Preheat oven to 375° F., and adjust the racks to divide the oven into thirds. Butter 2 cookie sheets, or line them with foil. Sift the flour, or flours, before measuring and resift with the baking powder, baking soda, salt and spices. Cream the butter until soft. Beat in both sugars until light and fluffy. Beat in the egg and the carrots. Stir in the vanilla and lemon extracts and the grated lemon rind. Gradually add the sifted dry ingredients until just incorporated. Fold in the nuts. Using a spoon and a rubber spatula, or 2 spoons, place rounded teaspoons of the dough about 2 inches apart on the cookie sheets.

Bake for 12 to 15 minutes, until the tops are golden and spring back when gently pressed with a fingertip. After about 8 minutes, reverse the sheets from the upper to the lower rack and turn them from front to back. Transfer to a rack to cool.

YIELD: 60 cookies

Yogurt Cocoa Drops

1¾ cups sifted all-purpose flour
½ teaspoon baking soda
¼ teaspoon salt
¼ pouı.d (1 stick) unsalted butter
½ cup firmly packed dark brown
  sugar

½ cup granulated sugar
1 egg
1 teaspoon vanilla extract
½ cup unsweetened cocoa powder
2/3 cup yogurt or buttermilk
1 cup chopped walnuts or almonds

Sift the flour before measuring and resift it with the baking soda and salt. Cream the butter with both sugars until light and smooth. Beat in the egg and vanilla extract. Beat in the cocoa. Alternately add the sifted dry ingredients and the yogurt by thirds until the flour is just incorporated. Fold in the nuts. Chill the dough for at least 1 hour.

Preheat oven to 400°F., and adjust the racks to divide the oven into thirds. Butter 2 cookie sheets, or line them with foil. Using a spoon and a rubber spatula, or 2 spoons, drop the batter by lightly rounded teaspoons 2 inches apart on the prepared sheets.

Bake for 8 to 10 minutes. About halfway through the baking time reverse the pans from the upper to the lower racks and turn them from front to back. Cookies will be slightly soft to the touch. Transfer to a rack to cool.

YIELD: 40 cookies

Walnut Clusters

The original recipe called for black walnuts. If you do not like their very special taste, substitute your favorite nut.

1½ ounces (1½ squares) unsweetened chocolate
½ cup sifted all-purpose flour
½ teaspoon salt
¼ teaspoon baking powder
2 ounces (½ stick) unsalted butter

½ cup granulated sugar
1 egg
1 teaspoon vanilla extract
1½ cups black walnuts or other nuts in large pieces

Preheat oven to 350°F., and adjust the racks to divide the oven into thirds. Butter 2 cookie sheets, or line them with foil. Melt the chocolate in a small bowl set in a larger pan of boiling water off heat. Sift the flour before measuring and resift it with the salt and baking powder. Cream the butter with the sugar until very light and fluffy. Beat in the egg and vanilla. Stir in the melted chocolate. Beat in the sifted dry ingredients and blend well. Lastly fold in the nuts. Using a spoon and a rubber spatula, or 2 spoons, drop the dough by teaspoons about 1½ inches apart on the prepared cookie sheets.

Bake for 10 to 12 minutes. After 6 or 7 minutes reverse the cookie sheets from the upper to the lower racks and turn them from front to back. Transfer to a rack to cool. Cookies will be soft to the touch. Don't overbake them.

YIELD: **30 cookies**

Benne Seed Wafers

*These cookies are usually described as originating in Charleston, South Carolina,
and appear in many cookbooks. Benne seeds are sesame seeds; the name of benne
was given to them in Africa and the name was carried to the Western Hemisphere
by the blacks who were brought here as slaves. "Benne" is commonly used for
"sesame" in the South and the islands of the West Indies. Sesame, or benne, is
among the world's oldest spice and oil-seed crops and it plays a part in the cuisine
of many lands. References to sesame go back to Egyptian tomb drawings long
before the days of Cleopatra. We know now that sesame (as an oil or in seed form)
is an important source of protein.*

4 ounces sesame seeds (¾ cup)
1¼ cups sifted all-purpose flour
½ teaspoon baking powder
¼ teaspoon salt
6½ ounces (1 1/3 sticks) unsalted
  butter

1½ cups firmly packed dark brown
  sugar
2 eggs, beaten
1 teaspoon vanilla extract

Preheat oven to 325°F., and adjust the racks to divide the oven into
thirds. Butter 2 cookies sheets, or line them with foil. Toast the
sesame seeds in a large heavy skillet, shaking and stirring them
until they are lightly browned. Immeditely remove them from the
pan and set them aside to cool slightly. Sift the flour before
measuring and resift it with the baking powder and salt. Cream
the butter until soft. Gradually beat in the brown sugar until light
and fluffy. Beat in eggs and vanilla. Gradually add the sifted flour
mixture and finally the sesame seeds. Using a spoon and a rubber
spatula, or 2 spoons, place level teaspoons of the dough about 3
inches apart on the prepared cookie sheets.
    Bake for 10 to 12 minutes, or until cookies are lightly browned at
the edges. After 7 minutes, reverse the cookie sheets from the
upper to the lower racks and turn them from front to back. After
removing the baked cookies from the oven, let them stand for
about ½ minute to firm up slightly. Then transfer to a rack to cool.

YIELD: 60 cookies
NOTE: This cookie dough is quite soft. If you prefer, chill it slightly,
form into a log, and slice for baking.

Florentines

A European classic with great elegance.

1/3 cup granulated sugar
1/3 cup heavy cream
1/3 cup honey
3 Tablespoons unsalted butter
1/3 cup candied orange peel, *or* 1/3
    cup mixed candied peel and candied
    cherries, finely chopped or ground

4 ounces blanched almonds, sliced
    or slivered (1 cup)
4 Tablespoons sifted all-purpose
    flour
6 ounces semisweet chocolate
1 Tablespoon vegetable shortening

Preheat oven to 400°F. Butter 2 cookie sheets heavily, or line them with foil. In a heavy saucepan over low heat combine the sugar, cream, honey and butter. Stir only until the sugar is dissolved. Increase the heat and boil the mixture, without stirring, until it reaches 238°F., on a candy thermometer or soft-ball stage (a ball should form when a bit of the mixture is dropped into cold water). Remove the pan from the heat and let it cool for about 5 minutes. Stir in the orange peel, almonds and flour. Using a spoon and a rubber spatula, or 2 spoons, place rounded teaspoons of the batter 3 inches apart on the prepared cookie sheets. Flatten each mound with a fork dipped into cold milk.

Bake for 8 to 10 minutes, or until golden brown. After about 6 minutes, reverse the baking sheets from upper to lower racks and turn them front to back. The cookies spread and are very soft. When they are done, remove one sheet from the oven, leaving the oven door open and the second sheet of cookies in the turned off oven. While the cookies are still warm and soft, pull them back into shape with a greased 3 inch round cookie cutter. Remove the second baking sheet from the oven and reshape the cookies. Leave the cookies on the baking sheets until they are firm enough to transfer to a rack to cool.

Melt the chocolate and stir in the shortening. When the cookies have cooled completely, place them bottom side up on a sheet of wax paper. Hold the cookies steady with a fork or a very long needle or skewer and spread the chocolate on the bottom or flat side. Refrigerate the cookies just long enough to set the chocolate.

YIELD: 20 cookies

Colonial Coriander Cookies

Coriander seeds were used extensively in baking in Colonial times in America. They lend an unusual flavor, pungent and slightly lemony. This recipe is adapted from an old one.

2 cups sifted all-purpose flour
½ teaspoon salt
¼ teaspoon baking soda
2 teaspoons ground coriander seeds
  (see NOTE)
½ teaspoon ground cinnamon

¼ pound (1 stick) unsalted butter
¾ cup light brown sugar
1 egg
½ cup yogurt, buttermilk or sour milk

Preheat oven to 375°F., and adjust the racks to divide the oven into thirds. Butter 2 cookies sheets or line them with foil. Sift the flour before measuring and resift it with the salt, baking soda, coriander (see Note) and cinnamon. Cream the butter and the sugar until soft and light. Add the egg, beating well. If you have ground the coriander yourself, add it now. Gradually add the sifted dry ingredients, alternating with the yogurt or buttermilk, and blend until just mixed. Using a spoon and a rubber spatula, or 2 spoons, place level teaspoons of the dough about 2 inches apart on the prepared cookie sheets, smoothing them into even rounds.

   Bake for about 15 minutes, or until lightly browned around the edges. Transfer to a rack to cool.

YIELD: 48 cookies
VARIATION: If you want to roll the dough and cut it into shapes, it should be wrapped and refrigerated for several hours before rolling.
NOTE: Coriander seeds come whole and ground. If you grind the seeds yourself in a mortar with a pestle, they will probably not be fine enough to go through the sifter and should be added later, where indicated.

Currant Tea Biscuits

A simple English biscuit (cookie to us) which is just as nice with milk or coffee as it is with a cup of tea.

1¼ cups sifted all-purpose flour
½ teaspoon baking powder
¼ teaspoon salt
¼ teaspoon ground nutmeg
¼ pound (1 stick) unsalted butter
½ cup granulated sugar

2 eggs beaten with 2 Tablespoons honey and 2 Tablespoons milk
½ teaspoon vanilla extract, *or* 1 teaspoon rosewater
1 Tablespoon brandy (optional)
2/3 cup dried currants

Preheat oven to 375°F., and adjust the racks to divide the oven into thirds. Butter 2 cookie sheets, or line them with foil. Sift the flour before measuring and resift it with the baking powder, salt and nutmeg. Cream the butter until soft. Beat in the sugar until light and fluffy. Stir in the egg beaten with the honey and milk, beating until well mixed. Add the vanilla or rosewater and brandy if you use it. Gradually add the sifted dry ingredients until just incorporated. Fold in the currants. Using a teaspoon and a rubber spatula, or the back of a second spoon, place teaspoons of the dough about 3 inches apart on the prepared sheets.

Bake for 8 to 10 minutes, or until the edges are lightly browned. After about 5 minutes, reverse the sheets from the upper to the lower racks, and turn them from front to back.

YIELD: 48 biscuits
VARIATION: If you should happen to have tiny tart tins, you would be following tradition to bake the dough in them.

Essie's Special Cookies

Essie lives in the lovely old Vermont town of Dorset, where she has been justifiably famous for these cookies for some years. Essie says "No one can eat just one."

1 cup sifted all-purpose flour	1 egg
½ teaspoon salt	1 teaspoon vanilla extract
½ teaspoon baking soda	1½ cups Kellogg's Special "K" cereal
¼ pound (1 stick) unsalted butter	½ cup raisins, preferably golden
2/3 cup granulated sugar	

Preheat oven to 350°F., and adjust the racks to divide the oven into thirds. Butter 2 baking sheets, or line them with foil. Sift the flour before measuring and resift it with the salt and baking soda. Cream the butter until light; gradually beat in the sugar. Add the egg, beating well, and stir in the vanilla. Gradually add the sifted dry ingredients and lastly the cereal and raisins. Mix well. Using a spoon and a rubber spatula, or 2 spoons, place slightly rounded teaspoons of the batter 2 inches apart on the prepared sheets. Flatten the mounds well with the back of a fork which has been dipped into cold water to prevent sticking.

Bake for 10 to 12 minutes, or until brown and crisp. After 6 or 7 minutes, reverse the baking sheets from the upper to the lower racks and turn them from front to back. Remove cookies from the pan immediately and cool on a rack.

YIELD: 50 cookies

Coconut Lemon Mounds

These are soft and chewy with a nice lemon tang. This recipe is rather loosely based on one of Mrs. Beeton's.

2 extra large eggs
1 cup granulated sugar
Grated rind of 1 lemon

7 ounces shredded or flaked coconut,
   (2 cups packed down)
½ cup sifted all-purpose flour

Preheat oven to 325°F., and adjust the racks to divide the oven into thirds. Butter and flour 2 cookie sheets, or line them with foil or parchment paper. Beat the eggs until very light. If you have a food processor, combine the sugar and pieces of lemon rind in the work bowl. Process them with the steel knife until the lemon rind is grated. Add the sugar, or sugar and lemon rind, to the eggs and continue to beat until the mixture is light, soft and creamy. It will look almost like a soft mayonnaise and should form a ribbon when dropped from a beater. Fold in the coconut, and the grated lemon rind if you have not added it previously. Sift the flour before measuring and resift it gradually into the batter, folding it in with a spatula or wooden spoon until just incorporated. Using a spoon and a rubber spatula, or 2 spoons, place slightly rounded teaspoons of the dough about 1 inch apart on the cookie sheets. Don't flatten them but rather leave them mounded.

Bake for 18 to 22 minutes, until the coconut is a light toasty brown. After about 12 minutes, reverse the cookie sheets from the upper to the lower racks and turn them from front to back. Transfer them to a rack to cool.

YIELD: 36 cookies
VARIATION: Substitute orange rind and add a few drops of orange extract.

Fudge Crisps

Thin, crisp and very chocolate tasting, these are for the chocolate lovers. Bake them plain or topped with nuts.

¼ pound (1 stick) unsalted butter
3 ounces (3 squares) unsweetened
   chocolate
1 cup granulated sugar
2 egg yolks
1 cup sifted all-purpose flour

1 teaspoon vanilla extract
2 teaspoons brandy, orange liqueur
   or rum (optional)
Slivered almonds or walnut halves
   (optional)

Preheat oven to 350°F., and adjust the racks to divide the oven into thirds. Line 2 cookie sheets with aluminum foil. In a small heavy saucepan over very low heat, or in the top part of a double boiler over hot water, combine the butter, cut into bits, and the chocolate. When chocolate is melted, remove pan from the heat to cool. In a mixing bowl, beat the sugar with the egg yolks until smooth. Thoroughly beat in the melted chocolate and butter. Gradually add the sifted flour, beating until just incorporated. Stir in the vanilla, and the liqueur if you use it. Using a teaspoon and a rubber spatula, or 2 spoons, place rounded teaspoons of the dough about 1½ inches apart on the cookie sheets. Flatten slightly, if desired, and top with a slivered almond or walnut half. Or the dough can be chilled briefly, then formed into balls 1 inch in diameter. Flatten them into 1½ inch rounds and top with the nuts if you use them.

Bake for about 15 minutes. After about 8 minutes, reverse the cookie sheets from the upper to the lower rack and turn them from front to back. They are done when the tops spring back very slightly when pressed with a fingertip. Carefully transfer to a rack to cool. They are soft when warm and crisp as they cool.

YIELD: 40 cookies
VARIATIONS: Form the dough into a log 1½ inches in diameter and about 12 inches long. Chill until firm enough to slice (less than an hour). Cut into slices ⅛ inch thick. Bake for about 12 minutes, reversing the racks after about 7 minutes. This makes about 66 cookies.

Instead of topping the cookies with nuts, fold in 1 cup chopped nuts when mixing the dough.

Your Grandmother's Molasses Cookies

There are two reasons for the name of these cookies. One is that both my grandmothers died long before I was born so I never knew them. The other reason is that anyone who tastes these cookies says that they are the kind made by his or her grandmother! This makes a big batch.

4¾ cups sifted all-purpose flour
1 Tablespoon baking soda
1 Tablespoon ground ginger
2 teaspoons ground cinnamon
1 teaspoon dry mustard
1 teaspoon ground cloves
½ teaspoon salt
1 Tablespoon instant coffee powder

½ pound (2 sticks) unsalted butter
1 cup granulated sugar
1 cup unsulfured molasses
1 egg
2/3 cup milk or very strong coffee
  (if coffee, omit the instant coffee)
1 1/3 cups raisins or dried currants,
  plumped

Preheat oven to 375°F., and adjust the racks to divide the oven into thirds. Line 2 cookie sheets with foil. Sift the flour before measuring and resift it with the baking soda, spices and salt. Stir in the instant coffee if you are using it. Cream the butter until soft. Gradually beat in the sugar until creamy and light. Beat in the molasses and egg. Alternately add the flour and milk or coffee, beating the batter well for about 30 seconds. Stir in the raisins. Using a spoon and a rubber spatula, or 2 spoons, place heaping teaspoons of the dough 2 inches apart on the prepared cookie sheets or on extra sheets of foil. Flatten cookies with the wet bottom of a small glass, or with a flat spatula repeatedly dipped into cold water, forming nice rounds.

Bake for about 18 minutes, until the tops spring back when gently pressed with a fingertip. After about 10 minutes, reverse the sheets from the upper to the lower racks and turn them from front to back. Slide the foil off the cookie sheets, and slide the cookie sheets under the next prepared foil sheets; continue baking the rest of the batch. Let the baked cookies remain on the foil for a minute or two before transferring them to a rack to cool.

YIELD: 90 rounds, 2½-inch size
VARIATIONS: For big cookies, use heaping tablespoons of the dough to make about 30 rounds.

For giant cookies, use a level ¼-cup measure of the dough to make about 18 rounds.

Lemon Wafers I

These plain and simple cookies have a delicate lemon flavor.

2¼ cups sifted all-purpose flour
½ teaspoon baking powder
Pinch of ground ginger
½ pound (2 sticks) unsalted butter
2/3 cup granulated sugar

3 Tablespoons lemon juice
Grated rind of 1 large lemon
3 egg whites
¼ teaspoon salt

Preheat oven to 375°F., and adjust the racks to divide the oven into thirds. Butter 2 cookie sheets, or line them with foil. Sift the flour before measuring and resift it with the baking powder and ginger. Cream the butter and sugar until light and fluffy, and beat in the lemon juice and rind. Beat the egg whites briefly with the salt and add them to the butter and sugar, beating them in vigorously. Very gently, stir in the flour. Using a spoon and a rubber spatula, or 2 spoons, place teaspoons of the dough about 2 inches apart on the prepared cookie sheets.

Bake for 10 to 12 minutes, until the edges are lightly browned. After about 6 minutes, reverse the cookies from the upper to the lower rack and turn them from front to back. Transfer to wire racks to cool.

YIELD: 50 cookies

Lemon Wafers II

A slightly different version of a favorite cookie, this one is made with whole eggs. It also has a bit of mace as its spice. Mace and nutmeg come from the same tropical fruit; the pit of the fruit contains the seed, which is nutmeg. The red membrane surrounding this seed is mace; it is much like nutmeg in flavor but more pungent.

2¼ cups sifted all-purpose flour
½ teaspoon baking powder
¼ teaspoon ground mace
¼ teaspoon salt
¼ pound (1 stick) unsalted butter

1 cup granulated sugar
3 eggs
Grated rind of 1 lemon
3 Tablespoons lemon juice

Preheat oven to 375°F., and adjust the racks to divide the oven into thirds. Butter 2 cookie sheets, or line them with foil. Sift the flour before measuring and resift it with the baking powder, mace and salt. Cream the butter with the sugar until light and fluffy. Add the eggs one at a time, beating after each addition. Stir in lemon rind and juice. Gradually add the sifted flour mixture. Using a spoon and a rubber spatula, or 2 spoons, place teaspoons of the dough 2 inches apart on the prepared cookie sheets.

Bake for about 15 minutes, or until the edges are lightly browned. After about 10 minutes, reverse the cookie sheets from the upper to the lower racks and turn them from front to back. Transfer to wire racks to cool.

YIELD: 50 cookies

Lemon Pecan Wafers

These are semisoft cookies, with a lovely lemon flavor. They are traditional Louisiana cookies.

2¾ cups sifted all-purpose flour
1 teaspoon baking soda
¼ teaspoon salt
½ pound (2 sticks) unsalted butter
½ cup granulated sugar
½ cup firmly packed light brown sugar

1 whole egg
2 extra egg yolks
3 Tablespoons lemon juice
Grated rind of 1 large lemon
3 ounces pecans, cut into medium-size pieces or chopped fine (see NOTE)

Preheat oven to 350°F., and adjust the racks to divide the oven into thirds. Butter 2 cookie sheets, or line them with foil. Sift the flour before measuring and resift it with the baking soda and salt. Cream the butter until soft. Add both sugars and beat until light and fluffy. Add the whole egg and the yolks and beat well. Add lemon juice and rind. Gradually add the sifted dry ingredients, beating only until the mixture is smooth. Fold in the nuts. Using a spoon and a rubber spatula, or 2 spoons, place rounded teaspoons of the dough 2 inches apart on the prepared cookie sheets.

Bake for 18 to 20 minutes, or until the edges are lightly browned. After about 10 minutes, reverse the cookie sheets from the upper to the lower rack and turn them from front to back. Transfer to a rack to cool.

YIELD: 72 cookies
NOTE: If you prefer to form the dough into 2 logs and chill and slice it, the nuts should be ground fine. Cut the chilled dough into ⅛-inch slices. Bake in a 350°F. oven for 12 to 15 minutes. After 9 minutes, reverse cookie sheets from upper to lower rack and turn from front to back.

Sesame-Seed Peanut-Butter Cookies

A great combination that everyone seems to enjoy.

2½ ounces sesame seeds (½ cup)
1 cup sifted all-purpose flour
1 teaspoon baking powder
¼ teaspoon baking soda
¼ teaspoon salt
½ teaspoon ground nutmeg

¼ pound (1 stick) unsalted butter
1 cup firmly packed light brown
    sugar
1 egg
½ cup creamy peanut butter

Preheat oven to 375°F., and adjust the racks to divide the oven into thirds. Line 2 cookie sheets with foil, or leave them plain. Toast the sesame seeds in a heavy pan or skillet, shaking and stirring them until they are lightly browned. Immediately remove them from the pan and set them aside to cool slightly. Sift the flour before measuring and resift it with the baking powder, baking soda, salt and nutmeg. Stir in 4 tablespoons of the sesame seeds. Cream the butter with the sugar until light and soft. Add the egg, beating it in well, and mix in the peanut butter. Gradually add the sifted dry ingredients. Using a spoon and a rubber spatula, or 2 spoons, place lightly rounded teaspoons of the dough 2 inches apart on the prepared cookie sheets. Flatten them with a fork dipped into cold water and sprinkle the tops of the cookies with the remaining sesame seeds.

Bake for 10 to 12 minutes, until edges have browned lightly. After about 6 minutes, reverse the cookie sheets from the upper to the lower rack and turn them from front to back. Don't let cookies get too dark.

YIELD: 40 cookies
NOTE: I think the cookies look neater and nicer if they are formed into 1-inch balls, then placed on the cookie sheets and flattened.

Stove-Top Peanut-Butter Crisps

These are quick and easy to make and require no baking — nice on a hot day.

¼ cup granulated sugar
½ cup peanut butter
½ cup light corn syrup

2 cups cornflakes
1 cup shredded coconut

In a large heavy saucepan over low heat, or in the top part of a double boiler over boiling water, combine the sugar, peanut butter and corn syrup. Bring just to a boil, stirring constantly until the sugar is dissolved. Add the cornflakes and coconut. Turn the heat to low. Drop tablespoons of the mixture onto wax paper and let cool.

YIELD: 40 crisps

Nutty Peanut-Butter Chocolate Chips

An increasingly popular cookie, and one of the stars of the cookie shops that are flourishing these days. This is a big batch but the recipe may be halved.

3 cups sifted all-purpose flour
1½ teaspoons baking soda
½ pound (2 sticks) unsalted butter
1 cup granulated sugar
1 cup firmly packed light brown sugar
1 teaspoon vanilla extract

2 eggs
1 cup smooth peanut butter
4 ounces salted peanuts, finely chopped (1 cup)
6 ounces semisweet chocolate morsels

Preheat oven to 375°F., and adjust the racks to divide the oven into thirds. Line 2 cookie sheets with foil, or leave them plain. Sift the flour before measuring and resift it with the baking soda. Cream the butter until soft. Add both the sugars and the vanilla, and beat until light and fluffy. Add the eggs one at a time, beating well after each addition. Beat in the peanut butter. Gradually add the sifted flour and baking soda. The mixture will be stiff. Stir in chopped peanuts and chocolate bits. Using a spoon and a rubber spatula, or 2 spoons, place rounded teaspoons of the dough about 2½ inches apart on the prepared cookie sheets. Flatten cookies slightly with the back of a fork dipped into cold water; they should be about ½-inch thick.

Bake for about 12 minutes, or until light brown. After about 8 minutes, reverse the cookie sheets from the upper to the lower racks and turn them from front to back. Transfer to a rack to cool.

YIELD: 96 cookies

Almond Chocolate Chips

½ cup sifted all-purpose flour
½ teaspoon ground cinnamon
¼ teaspoon salt
Pinch of ground nutmeg
1½ cups ground blanched almonds

3 eggs, lightly beaten
½ cup sugar
⅛ teaspoon almond extract
6 ounces semisweet chocolate chips

Preheat oven to 350°F., and adjust the racks to divide the oven into thirds. Lightly butter 2 cookie sheets, or line them with foil. Sift the flour before measuring and resift with the cinnamon, salt and nutmeg. Stir in the almonds and set this aside. Beat the eggs and sugar until the mixture is light and pale. Add the almond extract. Stir in the flour and almond mixture until thoroughly blended. Stir in the chocolate bits. Using a teaspoon and a small rubber spatula, or the back of another spoon, drop the batter by slightly rounded teaspoons about 1½ inches apart onto the cookie sheets.

Bake for about 12 minutes. About halfway through the baking time, reverse the cookie sheets from upper to lower racks and turn them from front to back. Cookies are done when they are lightly brown and almost firm. Remove from cookie sheets and cool on racks.

YIELD: 36 cookies

Butterscotch Chocolate Chips

These are moist and chewy with that special flavor that comes from the brown sugar.

2/3 cup sifted all-purpose flour
½ teaspoon baking powder
¼ teaspoon salt
¼ pound (1 stick) unsalted butter

1 cup lightly packed dark brown sugar
1 egg, lightly beaten
1 teaspoon vanilla extract
6 ounces semisweet chocolate bits

Preheat oven to 375°F., and adjust the racks to divide the oven into thirds. Lightly butter 2 cookie sheets, or line them with foil. Sift the flour before measuring and resift it with the baking powder and salt. Cream the butter with the brown sugar until it is smooth and light. Beat in the egg and vanilla. When thoroughly blended, add the flour gradually until it is just incorporated. Fold in the chocolate bits. Using a spoon and a rubber spatula, or 2 spoons, drop the dough by lightly rounded teaspoons about 1½ inches apart on the prepared cookie sheets.

Bake them for 8 to 10 minutes. About halfway through the baking time, reverse the cookie sheets from the upper to the lower rack and turn them from front to back. Cookies are done when they spring back when gently pressed with a fingertip. Remove from the sheet and cool on a rack.

YIELD: about 36 cookies

Chocolate Chocolate-Chip Cookies

Satisfyingly chocolate-saturated to soothe the chocoholics.

2 cups sifted all-purpose flour
½ teaspoon baking soda
6 ounces (1½ sticks) unsalted butter
1 cup granulated sugar, *or* ½ cup granulated sugar and ½ cup firmly packed brown sugar
2 eggs, lightly beaten
1 teaspoon vanilla extract

6 Tablespoons unsweetened cocoa powder
¼ cup yogurt, buttermilk or sour cream
6 ounces semisweet chococlate bits
¾ cup chopped walnuts or pecans (optional)

Preheat oven to 350°F., and adjust the racks to divide the oven into thirds. Line 2 cookie sheets with foil. Sift the flour before measuring and resift it with the baking soda. Cream the butter with the sugar (or sugars). Beat in the eggs and vanilla. Beat in the cocoa and mix thoroughly. Add the yogurt. Gradually add the flour mixture and beat until just mixed. Fold in the chocolate bits, and nuts if you use them. Using a spoon and a rubber spatula, or 2 spoons, place lightly rounded teaspoons of the dough on the cookie sheets, allowing about 1½ inches between them.

Bake for 12 to 15 minutes. About halfway through the baking time, reverse the cookie sheets from the upper to the lower racks and turn them from front to back. Cookies will still be soft to the touch. Wait a minute or two before transferring to a rack to cool.

YIELD: about 50 cookies

Orange Coconut Drops

The orange gives these a lovely tang and the coconut adds a little crunch.

2 cups sifted all-purpose flour
½ teaspoon baking soda
¼ teaspoon salt
½ teaspoon ground mace or nutmeg
6 ounces (1½ sticks) unsalted butter
1 cup granulated sugar

1 egg
1 teaspoon grated lemon rind
1½ teaspoons grated orange rind
1 Tablespoon orange juice
¾ cup sour cream or drained yogurt (see Note)
3½ ounces shredded or flaked coconut (about 1 cup)

Preheat oven to 375°F., and adjust the racks to divide the oven into thirds. Butter 2 cookie sheets, or line them with foil. Sift the flour before measuring and resift it with the baking soda, salt and mace. Cream the butter until soft. Beat in the sugar until light and fluffy. Add the egg and beat; then add both grated rinds and the orange juice. Add the flour and the sour cream or yogurt alternately until both are incorporated. Stir in the coconut. Using a spoon and a rubber spatula, or the back of a second spoon, drop rounded teaspoons of the dough about 2 inches apart on the prepared cookie sheets.

Bake for 12 to 14 minutes, until lightly colored. After 8 or 9 minutes, reverse the cookie sheets from the upper to the lower rack and turn them from front to back. Transfer to a rack to cool.

YIELD: 42 cookies
NOTE: If yogurt is drained for about 10 minutes, it becomes thick and similar to sour cream in consistency, at a much lower calorie count. One cup (8 oz.) yogurt will yield ¾ cup drained yogurt in about 10 minutes. Drain the yogurt through a coffee filter, through cheesecloth, or through a sieve lined with a paper towel.

Peppermint Chocolate Drops

Peppermint and chocolate go together beautifully in these drop cookies.

2 ounces (2 squares) unsweetened
  chocolate
2¼ cups sifted all-purpose flour
½ teaspoon salt
6 ounces (1½ sticks) unsalted butter

¾ cup granulated sugar
2 eggs
4 ounces crushed peppermint candy
  (see NOTE)

Melt the chocolate and set it aside to cool. Preheat oven to 350°F., and adjust the racks to divide the oven into thirds. Butter 2 cookie sheets, or line them with foil. Sift the flour before measuring and resift it with the salt. Cream the butter until soft. Beat in the sugar until light. Add the eggs one at a time, beating after each addition. Stir in the melted and cooled chocolate. Add the flour and salt, stirring it in well. Stir in the crushed peppermint candy.

Using a spoon and a rubber spatula, or the back of a second spoon, place teaspoons of the dough 1 inch apart on the prepared cookie sheets. Bake for 10 to 12 minutes; the top should spring back when gently pressed with a fingertip. Don't overbake. Transfer to a rack to cool.

YIELD: 60 cookies
VARIATION: Form the dough into a log 2 inches in diameter and chill until firm enough to slice. Cut into ¼-inch slices and bake for 8 to 10 minutes.
NOTE: Peppermint bits are usually sold in 8-ounce packages. One half of a package is the quantity called for, about 1 cup.

Ellen's Lace Cookies

Several years ago, when Ellen was about 14, these marvelous cookies were her contribution to a very special birthday brunch being given by her parents. I took one bite and demanded the recipe.
Don't try these on a wet or humid day!
P. S. Ellen's mother says the recipe really came from her friend Dorothy.

¼ pound (1 stick) unsalted butter
½ cup granulated sugar
½ cup ground blanched almonds

1 Tablespoon flour
2 Tablespoons cherry or orange liqueur

Preheat oven to 350°F., and adjust the racks to divide the oven into thirds. Butter and flour 2 cookie sheets and shake off the excess flour. Or line sheets with foil and cut extra pieces of foil the size of the cookie sheets. In a heavy saucepan or skillet combine the butter, sugar, almonds and flour. Place over moderate heat, stirring, until the butter is completely melted. Remove from heat and stir in the liqueur. Using a teaspoon and a rubber spatula, or the back of a second teaspoon, place teaspoons of the batter on the baking sheets, allowing 4 inches of space between the mounds; they spread a lot. Form additional cookies on 2 foil sheets.

Bake for 6 to 7 minutes, until golden brown and bubbly. Let them stand for no more than 1 minute before removing to a rack to cool. You can also curl these over a rolling pin or the handle of a wooden spoon while they are still warm and soft (for method, see English Brandy Snaps, p. 65). If they cool too fast to curl, return them to the oven briefly to soften. Cool them seam side down on a rack. Slide the cookie sheets under the filled foil pieces and continue baking and curling. Store airtight.

YIELD: 24 cookies

Swedish Oatmeal Cookies

The almond topping gives a distinctive flavor to these rich oatmeal cookies.

¾ cup sifted all-purpose flour
½ teaspoon baking soda
¼ teaspoon salt
¼ pound (1 stick) unsalted butter
1/3 cup granulated sugar

1/3 cup firmly packed dark brown
   sugar
1 egg
½ teaspoon vanilla extract
1½ cups old-fashioned rolled oats

Topping

¼ cup granulated sugar
2 ounces (½ stick) unsalted butter
1 Tablespoon light corn syrup

1/3 cup chopped blanched almonds
⅛ teaspoon almond extract
   (optional)

Preheat oven to 350°F., and adjust the racks to divide the oven into thirds. Line 2 cookie sheets with foil. Sift the flour before measuring and resift it with the baking soda and salt. Cream the butter. Gradually add both sugars and mix well. Add the egg and vanilla and beat well. Gradually add the flour mixture and finally the rolled oats; mix well. Using a spoon and a rubber spatula, or 2 spoons, place rounded teaspoons of dough on the cookie sheets, allowing about 2 inches between the mounds.

Bake cookies for about 8 minutes. While they are baking, prepare the topping by combining the sugar, butter and corn syrup in a small heavy saucepan. Bring to a boil, remove from the heat, and stir in the chopped almonds and the almond extract if you use it. After 8 minutes, remove cookies from the oven but leave the oven turned on. Place a scant ½ teaspoon of the almond topping in the center of each cookie, pressing in slightly. Return the cookies to the oven, reversing the sheets from upper to lower racks and turning them from front to back. Bake for an additional 6 to 8 minutes, until cookies are golden brown. Reverse the sheets from front to back again if cookies are browning unevenly. Let cookies cool for a minute or so before removing from the sheets to cool on a rack.

YIELD: 36 cookies

English Brandy Snaps

These curled cookies are often served filled with sweetened whipped cream.

1 cup sifted all-purpose flour
1½ teaspoons ground ginger
½ cup light molasses, *or* ¼ cup dark
   molasses and ¼ cup light corn
   syrup

2/3 cup granulated sugar
¼ pound (1 stick) unsalted butter,
   cut into small bits
1 Tablespoon brandy

Preheat oven to 300°F., and adjust the racks to divide the oven into thirds. Butter 2 cookie sheets. Sift the flour before measuring and resift with the ginger. In a heavy-bottom saucepan heat the molasses, or molasses and corn syrup, with the sugar and cut-up butter until syrup is hot and the butter is melted. Remove from heat. Add the flour and ginger gradually, beating until smooth. As the mixture cools, it will thicken slightly. Beat in the brandy. Drop batter by teaspoons very far apart, placing about 6 mounds on a buttered standard cookie sheet. They will spread during baking.

Bake snaps for 10 to 12 minutes, until they are light brown. About halfway through the baking time, reverse the cookie sheets from the upper to the lower rack and turn them from front to back. If you are not practiced at curling cookies, you may prefer to bake 1 sheet at a time. In that case, place the single sheet at the center level of the oven. Remove the cookie sheets from the oven and let cookies cool for a minute before attempting to remove them, but you will need to work quickly while they are still warm. Remove one cookie at a time and place it face down on a work surface. Place the round handle of a wooden spoon at the edge of the cookie nearest you and loosely roll the cookie around the handle. Immediately slide the cookie off the handle and place it seam side down on a rack to cool. Continue to form the cookies in this fashion. If they cool too much and become too crisp, return them to the oven briefly.

If the cookies are to be filled, you will need a larger round than a spoon handle. Some hardware stores (and any lumberyard) sell wooden dowels 1 inch in diameter. The cookies soften easily and must be stored airtight to remain crisp. If they are to be filled, it should be done just before serving them.

YIELD: **about 36 snaps**

Molasses Yogurt Cookies

These are soft moist cookies with an old-fashioned flavor.

3½ cups sifted all-purpose flour
2 teaspoons baking soda
2 teaspoons ground ginger
1 teaspoon ground cinnamon
¼ teaspoon salt
6 ounces (1½ sticks) unsalted butter

½ cup granulated sugar
2 eggs, lightly beaten
¾ cup molasses
½ cup yogurt or buttermilk
1 cup raisins

Sift the flour before measuring and resift it with the baking soda, ginger, cinnamon and salt. Set it aside. In a bowl, cream the butter with the sugar until light and fluffy. Beat in the eggs. Combine molasses with yogurt or buttermilk. Alternately add the liquid and dry ingredients, one third at a time, until the flour is just incorporated. Fold in the raisins. Refrigerate the batter for 1 hour.

Preheat oven to 375°F., and adjust the racks to divide the oven into thirds. Lightly butter 2 cookie sheets, or line them with foil. Using a tablespoon and a rubber spatula, or the back of a second spoon, drop slightly rounded spoons of batter about 2 inches apart. Flatten them with the wet bottom of a small glass or with a flat spatula, dipped into cold water repeatedly.

Bake for 10 to 12 minutes. After 6 or 7 minutes reverse the cookie sheets from the upper to the lower rack and turn them from front to back. Cookies are done when they spring back when gently touched with a fingertip. Transfer them to a wire rack to cool.

YIELD: about 44 cookies

Chocolate Chunk Cookies

These were developed to please my friend Marilyn who wanted a "super" chocolate-chip cookie. These finally did it!

2½ cups sifted all-purpose flour
1 teaspoon baking powder
¼ teaspoon salt
6 ounces (1½ sticks) unsalted butter
¾ cup granulated sugar
¾ cup firmly packed brown sugar
1 egg

3 Tablespoons cream or half-and-half
1 teaspoon vanilla extract
12 ounces semisweet Swiss chocolate
   bars, cut into bits
1 cup chopped nuts — almonds,
   filberts, pecans or walnuts

Preheat oven to 375°F., and adjust the racks to divide the oven into thirds. Butter 2 baking sheets or line them with foil. Sift the flour before measuring and resift it with the baking powder and salt. Cream the butter with both sugars and add the egg, beating until light and fluffy. Beat in the cream and the vanilla. Add the sifted dry ingredients, blending them in, and fold in the chocolate pieces and nuts. Using a spoon and a rubber spatula, or 2 spoons, place lightly rounded ½ teaspoons of dough about 1 inch apart on the baking sheet.

Bake for 9 to 12 minutes, or until cookies are lightly browned at the edges. After 6 or 7 minutes, reverse the baking sheets from the upper to the lower racks and turn them from front to back. Transfer to a rack to cool.

YIELD: about 60 cookies

Parsnip Soybean Cookies

I think that if parsnips were a brand new vegetable called "white carrots" everyone would be eating them. However, there seems to be a terrible prejudice against this delicious vegetable. When I was testing these recipes, I never told anyone about the parsnips and they ate them happily. Afterward, many confessed that they would have declined if they had known! My advice to you is that you don't tell your friends until after they've eaten them.

1¾ cups sifted all-purpose flour
1 teaspoon baking powder
1 teaspoon baking soda
1 teaspoon ground ginger
½ teaspoon ground cinnamon
¼ teaspoon salt
¼ pound (1 stick) unsalted butter

1 egg
½ cup honey or molasses
1 cup shredded or grated raw parsnips
½ cup toasted soybeans
½ cup raisins

Preheat oven to 350°F., and adjust the racks to divide the oven into thirds. Butter 2 cookie sheets, or line them with foil. Sift the flour before measuring and resift it with the baking powder, baking soda, spices and salt. Cream the butter until very soft. Beat in the egg. Add the honey or molasses and beat in well. Beat in the parsnips. Gradually add the sifted dry ingredients, beating just until mixed. Stir in the soybeans and raisins. Using a teaspoon and a rubber spatula, or 2 spoons, place rounded teaspoons of the dough about 2 inches apart on the cookie sheets.

Bake for 12 to 15 minutes, until the cookies are golden in color and the tops spring back when lightly pressed with a fingertip. After about 8 minutes, reverse the sheets from the upper to the lower rack and turn them from front to back. Transfer to a rack to cool.

YIELD: 60 cookies

Squashed Rocks

Old-fashioned cookies were often called "rocks" because of their thick and lumpy shape, not due to their hardness. These spicy cookies are made with cooked winter squash or pumpkin.

2¼ cups sifted all-purpose flour
2 teaspoons baking powder
½ teaspoon baking soda
¼ teaspoon salt
1 teaspoon ground cinnamon
½ teaspoon ground nutmeg
½ teaspoon ground ginger
¼ teaspoon ground cloves
6 ounces (1½ sticks) unsalted butter

½ cup granulated sugar
½ cup firmly packed brown sugar
1 egg
1 cup mashed cooked winter squash
   or pumpkin (not pie mix)
Grated rind of 1 orange
1 cup raisins
1 cup chopped nuts

Preheat oven to 375°F., and adjust the racks to divide the oven into thirds. Butter 2 cookie sheets, or line them with foil. Sift the flour before measuring and resift it with the baking powder, baking soda, salt and spices. Cream the butter until very soft. Beat in both sugars until light and fluffy. Beat in the egg and the squash or pumpkin. Stir in the grated orange rind. Gradually add the sifted dry ingredients, beating them in just until incorporated. Fold in the raisins and nuts. Using a spoon and rubber spatula, or 2 spoons, place lightly rounded tablespoons of the dough about 1½ inches apart on the cookie sheets.

Bake for 15 to 18 minutes, until the tops are light brown and spring back when gently pressed with a fingertip. After about 10 minutes, reverse the sheets from the upper to the lower rack and turn them from front to back. Transfer to a rack to cool.

YIELD: 50 cookies

Oatmeal Applesauce Cookies

These are slightly soft and very satisfying.

2 cups sifted all-purpose flour
½ teaspoon baking soda
¼ teaspoon salt
½ teaspoon ground cinnamon
¼ teaspoon ground cloves
¼ teaspooon ground nutmeg
¼ pound (1 stick) unsalted butter

¾ cup firmly packed dark brown
  sugar
1 egg, lightly beaten
1½ cups old-fashioned rolled oats
1 cup applesauce
½ cup raisins

Preheat oven to 350°F., and adjust the racks to divide the oven into thirds. Butter 2 cookie sheets, or line them with foil. Sift the flour before measuring and resift it with the baking soda, salt and spices. Cream the butter with the sugar until soft and fluffy. Beat in the egg. Add the flour mixture, then the oats and applesauce; beat until very smooth. Stir in the raisins. Using a tablespoon with a rubber spatula, or another spoon, drop slightly rounded spoons of the batter about 2 inches apart on the cookie sheets.

   Bake for 12 to 15 minutes, until lightly browned. Remove from cookie sheets to cool on a rack.

YIELD: 40 cookies

Molded Cookies

Dry Cookie Mix
For a Refrigerator Cookie Mix, see page 94.

4½ cups sifted all-purpose flour
½ cup nonfat dry milk powder
3 cups granulated sugar

1½ Tablespoons baking powder
1 teaspoon salt

Sift the flour before measuring and place it in a large bowl. Add the other ingredients and stir well to mix thoroughly. Sift all the ingredients twice. Store in an airtight container.

YIELD: about 8 cups
NOTE: This should be used within a month for best results. Date the container so that you know when you mixed it.
TO USE DRY MIX: To 2 cups of dry mix, add 1 beaten egg and 3¼ ounces (2/3 stick) to ¼ pound (1 stick) melted butter and 1 teaspoon vanilla extract. Blend well. Using your hands which have been lightly floured, form into balls 1 inch in diameter. Place 2 inches apart on buttered or foil-lined baking sheets, flattening balls slightly if you wish.
VARIATIONS:
Add ½ cup raisins to dry mix before adding eggs, butter and vanilla.
Add ½ cup flaked coconut.
Add ½ cup semisweet chocolate bits.
Add ½ cup chopped nuts.
Add ¼ cup sifted unsweetened cocoa powder and use ¼ pound butter.

Snickerdoodles

Believed to be of Colonial origin, these cookies turn up in most cookie collections, partly because of the amusing name.

2½ cups sifted all-purpose flour
1 teaspoon baking powder
1 teaspoon baking soda
½ teaspoon salt
¼ pound (1 stick) unsalted butter
2 eggs

1 1/3 cups firmly packed light brown
   sugar
1 teaspoon vanilla extract
2 Tablespoons granulated sugar
   mixed with 2 teaspoons ground
   cinnamon (for topping)

Sift the flour before measuring and resift it with the baking powder, baking soda and salt. Cream the butter with the brown sugar and beat well. Add the eggs, one at a time, beating after each addition, and the vanilla. Gradually add the sifted dry ingredients, beating only until mixed. Wrap the dough in foil or plastic wrap and chill it for about 1 hour.

Preheat oven to 400°F., and adjust the racks to divide the oven into thirds. Remove chilled dough from refrigerator and form level teaspoons into balls. Roll the balls in the cinnamon sugar mixture. Place the balls 2 inches apart on an ungreased or foil-lined cookie sheet. Bake them for 10 to 12 minutes. About halfway through the baking time, reverse the cookie sheets from top to bottom and turn them from front to back. Cookies will be nicely browned.

YIELD: **60 cookies**
NOTE: Instead of forming the chilled dough into balls, rounded teaspoons of the dough can be dropped on the sheet. In that case, sprinkle the cinnamon sugar mixture on them.

Mariza's Coconut Balls

In Brazil, where both Mariza and the recipe originated, the coconut would always be fresh, but they are delicious even using dried coconut.

1 cup granulated sugar	2 cups flaked or shredded coconut
½ cup water	½ teaspoon lemon extract or vanilla
4 egg yolks	or almond extract
¼ cup sifted all-purpose flour	

Combine the sugar and water in a large heavy saucepan set over moderate heat. Stir until the sugar is completely dissolved. Continue to cook the syrup, without stirring, until it reaches 230° F. on a candy thermometer, or thread stage (a small amount of syrup dropped into ice water will form a thread). Remove the pan from the heat to cool slightly.

Beat the yolks lightly in a bowl and beat in the flour until mixed. Add about 2 tablespoons of the hot syrup, stirring constantly, then pour this mixture slowly into the pan of syrup. Add the coconut and return the pan to low heat, stirring constantly. Do not let it boil. Continue stirring until the mixture becomes very thick and stiff. Remove the pan from heat, stir in the lemon or other extract, and set it aside to cool completely.

Heat oven to 375°F., and adjust the racks to divide the oven into thirds. Butter 2 cookie sheets, or line them with foil. Form a coconut ball by rolling 1 tablespoon of the mixture between your hands. Continue until all dough is used. Place balls 1 inch apart on the prepared cookie sheets. Bake for about 14 minutes, or until they are golden brown. Halfway through the baking time, reverse the cookie sheets from the upper to the lower racks and turn them from front to back. Transfer to a rack to cool.

YIELD: 40 balls

Alice's Stove-Top Date Nut Balls

This quick and easy recipe comes from my friend Gail, whose grandmother Alice has been making these for years.

¾ cup granulated sugar
1 cup pitted dates, chopped
2 eggs, beaten
1 teaspoon vanilla extract

1 cup chopped nuts
3 cups rice breakfast crisps
1¼ cups shredded coconut

In a large heavy skillet or saucepan, combine the sugar, chopped dates and eggs. Cook over moderate heat for about 5 minutes, or until the mixture pulls away from the sides of the pan. Remove from heat and cool for 3 minutes or so. Stir in the vanilla, nuts and rice crisps. Wet your hands in cold water and form the date mixture into balls the size of walnuts. Roll each ball in coconut and cool on wax paper.

YIELD: 24 balls

Butterscotch Coconut Fingers

These are as good as they look — rich buttery-flavored fingers with toasted coconut ends.

4 cups sifted all-purpose flour
1 teaspoon baking powder
1 pound (4 sticks) unsalted butter
½ cup granulated sugar

½ cup firmly packed dark brown sugar
2 eggs, separated
½ cup shredded sweetened coconut

Sift the flour before measuring and resift it with the baking powder. Cream the butter until soft. Beat in both sugars until the mixture is light and creamy. Separate the eggs, reserving the whites. Beat the yolks lightly and then beat them into the butter and sugar. Gradually add the sifted flour and baking powder and stir until blended. Refrigerate the dough for about 2 hours.

Toast the coconut by placing it in a large heavy skillet over moderately low heat. Stir constantly with a wooden spoon to prevent burning; shreds should have a light brown toasty color in 3 or 4 minutes. Remove coconut from the pan and spread out on a sheet of wax paper or foil to cool.

Preheat oven to 350°F., and adjust the racks to divide the oven into thirds. Butter 2 cookie sheets, or line them with foil. Beat the egg whites until foamy. Work on one third of the dough at a time, keeping the balance refrigerated. Form a slightly rounded tablespoon of the dough into 3-inch finger by rolling it between your hands. Dip about 1 inch of each end into the reserved egg white; then roll the dipped ends in the toasted coconut. Continue until all dough is shaped and coated. Place the fingers about 2 inches apart on the prepared cookie sheets. Bake for 10 to 12 minutes, until pale golden in color. Transfer to a rack to cool.

YIELD: 72 cookies

Cardamom Coconut Wafers

Cardamom is native to India, where it is widely used in curries and desserts. It is almost as popular in Scandinavian countries, where it is extensively used in baking. The light-colored pods, about the size of a cranberry, hold up to 20 tiny, black aromatic seeds. The coconut in the following recipe suggests that the wafers are probably Indian in origin.

2¼ cups sifted all-purpose flour
1½ teaspoons baking powder
½ teaspoon salt
½ teaspoon ground cardamom
½ pound (2 sticks) unsalted butter

1¼ cups granulated sugar
2 eggs
1½ ounces flaked or chopped coconut
   (½ cup)

Preheat oven to 375°F. Use unbuttered cookie sheets or line them with foil. Sift the flour before measuring and resift it with the baking powder, salt and cardamom. Cream the butter with 1 cup of the sugar until light and fluffy. Add the eggs one at a time, beating after each addition. Gradually add the flour mixture, beating until just incorporated. Using a level teaspoon as a measure, form balls about ¾ inch in diameter and place them about 2 inches apart on the cookie sheets. With the bottom of a glass wrapped in damp cloth or paper towel, flatten them to a thickness of ⅛ inch. Combine remaining ¼ cup granulated sugar with the coconut and sprinkle on the tops of the rounds.

Bake for about 10 minutes, or until the edges are lightly browned. After about 6 minutes, reverse the cookie sheets from the upper to the lower rack and turn them from front to back. Let cookies stand for about ½ minute before transferring to a rack to cool.

YIELD: 72 rounds, 1¾ inches across

Ginger Crackles

These are crisp and dry and spicy.

2 cups sifted all-purpose flour
1 teaspoon baking soda
1½ teaspoons ground ginger
½ teaspoon ground nutmeg or mace
½ teaspoon ground cinnamon

¼ teaspoon ground cloves
6½ ounces (1 1/3 sticks) unsalted butter
2/3 cup sugar
¼ cup dark molasses
1 teaspoon vanilla extract

Sift the flour before measuring and resift it with the baking soda and all the spices. Cream the butter until soft. Beat in 1/3 cup of the sugar until light and fluffy. Stir in the molasses and vanilla. Gradually add the flour, mixing it well. Refrigerate the dough for an hour or so until it is firm.

Preheat oven to 375°F., and adjust the racks to divide the oven into thirds. Butter 2 cookie sheets, or line them with foil. Using a rounded teaspoon as a measure, roll bits of dough between your hands to form a ball about 1 inch in diameter, about the size of a large cherry. Roll the balls in the remaining sugar, flattening them slightly. Place the balls about 1½ inches apart on the prepared cookie sheets. Bake for 12 to 16 minutes, until the cookies are crackled on top and dry. After 7 or 8 minutes, reverse the cookie sheets from the upper to the lower racks and turn them from front to back. Transfer to a rack to cool.

YIELD: 48 cookies

Mexican Butter Cookies

With very slight variations, these are called mantecaditos *or* biscochitos *or* polvorones. *Some contain aniseeds, one version has none, and another version steeps the aniseeds in boiling water, using the water and discarding the seeds. They are all delicious and buttery.*

2 cups sifted all-purpose flour
½ teaspoon salt
1 teaspoon crushed aniseeds
½ pound (2 sticks) unsalted butter
¾ cups granulated sugar
1 egg

1½ teaspoons grated lemon rind *and* 1 teaspoon vanilla extract, *or* 1 Tablespoon brandy, rum or whiskey
4 Tablespoons granulated sugar mixed with 2 teaspoons ground cinnamon

Preheat oven to 325°F., and adjust the racks to divide the oven into thirds. Lightly butter 2 cookie sheets, or line them with foil. Sift the flour before measuring and resift it with the salt. Stir in the aniseeds. Cream the butter with the sugar until light. Beat in the egg and the lemon rind and vanilla if you use them. Gradually add the sifted flour, beating until just mixed. Finally beat in the brandy, if you use that. Using a rounded teaspoon as a measure, form balls about 1 inch in diameter by rolling them between your hands. Place them about 1½ inches apart on the prepared cookie sheets.

Bake for 20 to 25 minutes, or until firm. Cool slightly on the sheets. While still warm, roll them in the sugar and cinnamon mixture and place them on a rack to cool completely.

YIELD: 50 cookies

Naples Sugar Cookies

Naples, Florida, is the source of these plain and tempting sugar cookies.

2 cups sifted all-purpose flour	½ cup granulated sugar
½ teaspoon salt	½ cup powdered sugar
½ teaspoon baking soda	2 eggs
½ teaspoon cream of tartar	½ teaspoon vanilla extract
½ pound (2 sticks) unsalted butter	Granulated sugar for topping

Preheat oven to 375°F., and adjust the racks to divide the oven into thirds. Line 2 baking sheets with foil. Sift the flour before measuring and resift it with the salt, baking soda and cream of tartar. Cream the butter until light. Add both sugars gradually, beating until the mixture is very soft and fluffy. Add the eggs one at a time, beating well after each addition. Stir in the vanilla and gradually add the sifted dry ingredients, mixing just until they are incorporated. Using a teaspoon for measuring, roll dough into balls about 1 inch in diameter. Roll each ball in granulated sugar and place them about 2 inches apart on the prepared baking sheets. Dip the bottom of a glass into granulated sugar and press down on the balls to flatten them.

Bake for 9 to 12 minutes, or until the edges are lightly browned. After about 6 minutes reverse the cookie sheets from the upper to the lower racks and turn them from front to back. Transfer to a rack to cool.

YIELD: 50 cookies

New Orleans Porcupines

These sweet cookies are for the days when you're feeling very thin or very deprived.

2 Tablespoons unsalted butter
2 eggs
1 cup firmly packed light or dark brown sugar
1 cup chopped (unsugared) dried dates

1 Tablespoon all-purpose flour
1½ cups chopped pecans
3 cups shredded coconut, preferably unsweetened (see NOTE)

Preheat oven to 300°F., and adjust the racks to divide the oven into thirds. Melt the butter and set it aside. Beat the eggs well and gradually beat in the sugar, then the melted butter. Toss the dates with the tablespoon of flour. Add the floured dates and the pecans to the batter. Stir in 1 cup of the coconut. Spread out remaining coconut on a piece of wax paper or foil. Using a rounded teaspoon as a measure, make small balls of the batter and roll each one in coconut. Place the balls about 2 inches apart on unbuttered or foil-lined cookie sheets.

Bake for 25 to 30 minutes, or until cookies are just beginning to brown. After about 15 minutes, reverse the cookie sheets from the upper to the lower racks and turn them from front to back. Transfer to a rack to cool.

YIELD: 50 cookies
NOTE: If the coconut is sweetened, reduce the amount of brown sugar by 2 Tablespoons.

No-Bake Baby Snowballs

Perhaps these are more of a candy than a cookie but they are lovely with fruit for dessert. Very fast to make, they can be stored in the freezer and will defrost in a short time.

½ cup ricotta cheese
3½ ounces sweetened shredded coconut

2 Tablespoons granulated sugar
2 teaspoons ground cinnamon

Spread the ricotta out flat on a piece of wax paper and sprinkle the coconut on top. Using a fork for mixing, blend them thoroughly. By slightly rounded teaspoons, form the mixture into 1 inch balls by rolling them between your hands. Blend the sugar and cinnamon together in a very small bowl. Drop the coconut balls in the bowl and roll them, one by one, in the sugar mixture. Place the balls on a sheet of aluminum foil and place them in the freezer. Wrap them airtight if they are to be stored in the freezer for any length of time.

I think these are better semifrozen rather than merely chilled in the refrigerator. They are best, I feel, after 40 minutes if they are placed directly on the floor of the freezer; about 90 minutes if the foil is not in direct contact with the floor of the freezer. If solidly frozen, defrost them at room temperature for about 20 minutes before serving.

YIELD: 18 cookies

Peanut Butter Cookies

A long-time favorite. This recipe makes a big batch of them. If you prefer, you can also freeze half of the dough and bake half.

2¾ cups sifted all-purpose flour
1½ teaspoons baking soda
¼ teaspoon salt
¼ pound (1 stick) unsalted butter
1 cup granulated sugar

1 cup firmly packed brown sugar, light or dark
2 eggs
1 cup peanut butter, preferably crunchy
½ teaspoon vanilla extract

Sift flour before measuring and resift it with the baking soda and salt. Cream the butter until soft. Add both sugars and beat until light and fluffy. Add the eggs one at a time, beating well after each addition. Beat in the peanut butter and the vanilla. Gradually add the sifted dry ingredients until just blended. Refrigerate the dough for about 2 hours.

Preheat oven to 375°F., and adjust the racks to divide the oven into thirds. Butter 2 cookie sheets, or line them with foil. Using a lightly rounded teaspoon as a measure, shape the dough into 1-inch balls by rolling it between your hands. Place the balls 3 inches apart on the cookie sheets and flatten them lightly with a fork dipped into cold water. Make a crisscross design with the tines of the fork.

Bake the cookies for 10 to 12 minutes, or until golden in color. After about 6 minutes, reverse the cookie sheets from the upper to the lower rack and turn them from front to back. Cool on a rack.

YIELD: 72 cookies

Black Walnut Cookies

This cookie is for those who like the very special taste of black walnuts. To me they are the truffle of the nut world. Not everyone agrees.

2 cups sifted all-purpose flour
½ teaspoon baking soda
Pinch of salt
3 ounces (¾ stick) unsalted butter

1 cup firmly packed brown sugar
2 eggs, lightly beaten
1 cup shelled black walnuts, coarsely
 chopped

Preheat oven to 350°F., and adjust the racks to divide the oven into thirds. Sift the flour before measuring and resift it with the baking soda and salt. Cream the butter; add the sugar and beat well. Add the eggs, mixing well. Gradually add the sifted dry ingredients, beating just until mixed. Fold in the nuts. Form into walnut-size balls and place them about 2 inches apart on an ungreased or foil-lined cookie sheet. Flatten the balls with the back of a fork which should be dipped repeatedly into a glass of cold water.

Bake for 12 to 15 minutes. About halfway through the baking time, reverse the cookie sheets from upper to lower racks and turn them from front to back. The cookies will have an even golden color. Transfer to a rack to cool.

YIELD: 36 cookies, 2½-inch size cookies
NOTE: Some people dip the cookies into confectioners' sugar while they are still warm and redip them after they have cooled.

Chinese Almond Cookies

A delicately almond-flavored cookie which is somewhat crumbly.

2½ cups sifted all-purpose flour
¼ teaspoon salt
1½ teaspoons baking powder
½ cup ground almonds
6 ounces (1½ sticks) unsalted butter

½ cup sugar
1½ teaspoons almond extract
2 egg yolks, mixed with 1 Tablespoon
  water (for glaze)
25 to 30 whole blanched almonds

Preheat oven to 375°F., and adjust the racks to divide the oven into thirds. Sift the flour before measuring and resift it with the salt and baking powder. Mix the ground almonds in with the flour. In a mixing bowl, cream the butter with the sugar until fluffy. Add the almond extract. Add the flour and ground almonds and knead into a smooth dough. It will be crumbly and fairly dry. Break off pieces of the dough and form into balls about the size of a walnut. Flatten the balls into rounds and place them 1 inch apart on ungreased cookie sheets. Beat the egg yolks with the water and brush tops of the cookies with this glaze. Press one whole almond into the center of each cookie.

Bake in the preheated oven for 12 to 14 minutes, or until the cookies are a pale golden brown. About halfway through the baking time reverse the cookie sheets from the upper to the lower rack and turn them from front to back. Remove from the sheets and cool on racks.

YIELD: about 30 cookies, 2-inch size

Mocha Walnut Chews

2 cups sifted all-purpose flour
1½ teaspoons baking powder
½ teaspoon salt
¼ pound (1 stick) unsalted butter
1 1/3 cups sugar
1 teaspoon vanilla extract

2 eggs, lightly beaten
2 ounces (2 squares) unsweetened
  chocolate
1/3 cup prepared strong coffee
½ cup chopped walnuts
½ cup confectioners' sugar (optional)

Sift the flour before measuring and resift it with the baking powder and salt. Cream the butter with the sugar until light and fluffy. Add the vanilla and beaten eggs and mix well. Melt the chocolate in the coffee. Add chocolate to the batter, then gradually add the flour until well mixed. Fold in the nuts. Chill the dough for at least 2 hours.

Preheat oven to 350°F., and adjust the racks to divide the oven into thirds. Lightly butter 2 baking sheets, or line them with foil. Remove the dough from the refrigerator and with hands form it into balls approximately 1 inch in diameter. Roll balls in confectioners' sugar if you use it, and place them 2 to 3 inches apart on the prepared cookie sheets. Bake for 12 to 15 minutes. About halfway through the baking time, reverse the cookie sheets from the upper to the lower rack and turn them from front to back. Cookies will still be fairly soft to the touch. Wait about a minute or so before transferring them to a rack to cool.

YIELD: 36 cookies

Madeleines au Chocolat

This chocolate version of the classic madeleine would never have been dipped into tea or even served in the morning. For the more Proustian type, the kind his Aunt Leonie dipped into her lime-flower tea, see the variation at the end of the recipe.

2 teaspoons unsalted butter
1 Tablespoon all-purpose flour
2 ounces (½ stick) unsalted butter, melted and cooled
2 extra large eggs, at room temperature

½ cup granulated sugar, *or* 1/3 cup superfine sugar
¼ cup sifted all-purpose flour
¼ cup unsweetened cocoa powder
½ teaspoon vanilla extract

Preheat oven to 375°F., and adjust the racks to divide the oven into thirds. You will need 2 madeleine pans, each one containing 12 shell-shaped depressions about 3 inches long. If you have only one pan, halve the recipe and prepare one batch at a time. This batter is a *génoise* batter and must be popped into the oven immediately.

Melt the 2 teaspoons butter in a small pan and beat in the tablespoon of flour. Using a pastry brush, spread this evenly in the shell shapes of the pan; use a dry brush to remove any excess. Melt 2 ounces butter in another small pan and set it aside to cool slightly. If the eggs are cold, warm them briefly in a bowl of warm water. Many cooks place the eggs and the sugar in the mixing bowl and set the bowl over hot water before beating them together. The eggs will mount better and produce greater volume if they are warm. When the melted butter is added to the egg and sugar mixture, the butter should be tepid, not hot. The egg and sugar mixture should be slightly warm or it will congeal the melted butter.

Sift the flour before measuring it, then resift it with the cocoa onto a sheet of wax paper. Return the mixture to the sifter and set it aside on the paper. Beat the eggs well and gradually beat in the sugar, preferably with an electric mixer, beating until the volume has tripled and looks like a thick, soft mayonnaise, 8 to 10 minutes. Add the vanilla toward the end. Sift about one third of the flour and cocoa mixture onto the egg and sugar mixture and fold it in quickly with a rubber spatula, preferably a large one. Work rapidly so as not to deflate the batter. Alternately fold in small additions of the flour and cocoa mixture and small amounts of the melted butter, working quickly to incorporate them. Fill the prepared pans, using about 1 tablespoon of batter for each shell shape; they should be half full. Immediately place them in the preheated oven.

Bake the madeleines for about 12 minutes. They are done when they can be removed from their shells, using the tip of a knife to loosen them. If they are too soft and don't want to budge, return them to the oven for another minute or so. Unmold them onto a cooling rack, shell side up. Sprinkle with confectioners' sugar, if you wish. If some of them are not quite perfectly shaped, the sugar is a good camouflage.

YIELD: 24 madeleines

VARIATION: For the more classic madeleine, eliminate the cocoa and increase the flour to ½ cup. Increase the vanilla to 1 teaspoon and add the grated rind of 1 lemon.

For an authentic Proustian madeleine, the Madeleines de Commercy, the batter is heavier, more like a pound cake, and it rests for an hour before being baked. I refer you to *From Julia Child's Kitchen* (Alfred A. Knopf, 1975).

Cracker-Barrel Coconut Crisps

The real old-fashioned coconut cookie that used to be sold loose from a great big glass jar in city stores, or from a cracker barrel or a big gaily-painted tin canister in the country. Have a bite of nostalgia!

2 cups sifted all-purpose flour
¾ teaspoon baking powder
¼ teaspoon baking soda
Pinch of salt
¼ pound (1 stick) unsalted butter
1 cup firmly packed brown sugar

1 egg
2 Tablespoons honey or molasses
½ teaspoon vanilla extract
3½ ounces shredded coconut (about
    1 cup packed)

Sift the flour before measuring it and resift it with the baking powder, baking soda and salt. Cream the butter until light. Gradually add the sugar until creamy and smooth. Beat in the egg, then add the honey and vanilla and mix thoroughly. Gradually add the sifted dry ingredients, mixing well. Finally stir in the coconut. Chill the dough for 3 hours or more.

Preheat oven to 375°F., and adjust the racks to divide the oven into thirds. Butter and flour 2 baking sheets, shaking off the excess flour, or line them with foil. Using a heaping teaspoon of dough for each cookie, and working with floured hands, roll the dough into a cigar shape about 3 inches long. Place the "cigars" on the baking sheet, allowing 3 inches space between them. Flatten them as thin as you can with lightly floured hands to make mounds about ¼ inch thick and 2 inches wide. Dip a fork into flour and press the tines on the surface of each cookie to make 4 parallel lengthwise ridges.

Bake the cookies for 10 to 12 minutes, or until they are an even golden brown. After 6 or 7 minutes, reverse the baking sheets from the upper to the lower racks and turn them from front to back. Let cookies cool for a few seconds before transferring them to a rack to cool.

YIELD: 28 cookies

Refrigerator and Cut-Out Cookies

Plain Sugar Cookies

These simple cookies combine well with other more elaborate ones. You can add nuts to these.

2 cups sifted all-purpose flour	1 cup granulated sugar
½ teaspoon baking soda	2 egg yolks, beaten
¼ teaspoon salt	1 teaspoon lemon rind, *or* 1 teaspoon
¼ pound (1 stick) unsalted butter	vanilla extract
	1 Tablespoon heavy cream

Sift the flour before measuring and resift it with the baking soda and salt. Cream the butter until soft. Beat in the sugar, blending until soft and light. Beat in the egg yolks and the lemon rind or vanilla. Gradually add the sifted flour mixture alternately with the cream and beat just until incorporated. Spread the dough out on a long sheet of wax paper, and form it into a round log 2 inches in diameter. Wrap the log in wax paper and foil and chill it for several hours or overnight.

Preheat oven to 375°F., and adjust the racks to divide the oven into thirds. Butter 2 cookie sheets, or line them with foil. Unwrap the chilled dough log and cut crosswise into slices about ¼ inch thick. Place the rounds about 2 inches apart on the prepared cookie sheets. Bake for about 10 minutes, until the edges are just golden. After about 6 minutes, reverse the sheets from the upper to the lower rack and turn them from front to back. Remove from the sheets and cool on a rack.

YIELD: 44 cookies

VARIATIONS: Sprinkle with plain sugar or cinnamon sugar before baking. Fold in ½ cup chopped nuts.

NOTE: Rather than chill the dough in log form, it can be rolled out ¼ inch thick and cut into rounds or other shapes.

Refrigerator Cookie Mix

This makes a very good cookie dough that can be easily varied. It freezes well and is nice to have on hand since it's very quick to slice off and bake a small batch of cookies. For those with limited freezer space, there is a dry mix which can be stored for several weeks at room temperature, in an airtight container (see p. 73).

2½ cups sifted all-purpose flour
2 teaspoons baking powder
½ teaspoon salt
¼ pound (1 stick) unsalted butter

1¼ cups granulated sugar
2 eggs
1 teaspoon vanilla extract

Sift the flour before measuring and resift it with the baking powder and salt. Cream the butter and beat in the sugar until the mixture is light and fluffy. Beat in the eggs and vanilla. Add the sifted dry ingredients and blend well. Chill the dough until firm for easier handling. It can also be frozen and sliced.

Roll out the chilled dough on a lightly floured surface or between 2 sheets of wax paper. Roll the dough very thin, ⅛ inch, for crisp cookies, or thicker, as you wish. Cut out with a floured cookie cutter into desired shapes and place on a greased or foil-lined baking sheet. Bake in a preheated 375° F. oven for 8 to 10 minutes, or until the edges are lightly browned. Transfer to a rack to cool.

YIELD: about 50 thin cookies

VARIATIONS:

BUTTERSCOTCH COOKIES: Increase the butter to 6 ounces (1½ sticks). Substitute brown sugar for the granulated sugar and increase the amount to 1½ cups, firmly packed.

CHOCOLATE COOKIES: Add 2 ounces (2 squares) melted unsweetened chocolate or ½ cup unsweetened cocoa powder before adding the flour. Reduce the flour to 2 cups.

NUT COOKIES: Add about 2/3 cup finely chopped or ground nuts. Or brush the tops of the unbaked cookies with a beaten egg, egg yolk or egg white, and sprinkle with chopped nuts.

SEED COOKIES: Mix 2 or 3 teaspoons of caraway or sesame seeds in with the flour before blending it in. Or use 1 teaspoon of aniseeds, eliminate the vanilla, and use about 4 drops of anise oil.
Or brush the tops of the unbaked cookies with a beaten whole egg, egg yolk or egg white, and sprinkle with the seeds.

SUGAR COOKIES: Roll out the dough to ¼-or 1/3-inch thickness. Sprinkle the tops of the unbaked cookies with coarse sugar and a little ground cinnamon.

Anise Cookies

These thin, crisp cookies are for those who enjoy the special flavor of anise.

1¾ cups sifted all-purpose flour   ¾ cup sugar
1½ teaspoons baking powder   1 egg
¼ teaspoon salt   Few drops of anise extract (optional)
¼ pound (1 stick) unsalted butter   1 teaspoon crushed aniseeds

Sift the flour before measuring and resift it with the baking powder and salt. Set it aside. Cream the butter with the sugar until light and fluffy. Beat in the egg and the anise extract if you use it. Add the flour gradually and beat just until it is incorporated. Stir in the aniseeds. Place a long piece of wax paper on the work surface. With a spatula, scrape the mixture from the bowl and spread it lengthwise on the paper to form a strip of dough about 12 inches or so long. Fold up the sides of the paper and press it against the dough. Then with your hands shape the dough into a roll about 2 inches in diameter, either round or oval. Wrap in more wax paper or foil and place on a cookie sheet in the refrigerator or preferably the freezer overnight.

Preheat oven to 400°F., and adjust the racks to divide the oven into thirds. Using a thin, very sharp knife, slice the log into ¼-inch-thick rounds. Place them about 1 inch apart on a foil-lined or ungreased cookie sheet. Bake them for 8 to 10 minutes, or until golden brown. About halfway through the baking time, reverse the cookie sheets from upper to lower racks and turn them from front to back. Remove from the sheet and cool on a rack.

YIELD: about 44 cookies

Cinnamon Orange Crisps

The bran flakes give an extra crunch to these.

1½ cups sifted all-purpose flour
1 teaspoon baking powder
1 teaspoon ground cinnamon
¼ teaspoon salt
¼ pound (1 stick) unsalted butter
1 cup firmly packed dark brown
   sugar

1 egg
1 Tablespoon coarsely grated orange
   rind
½ cup bran flakes
¼ cup chopped pecans

Sift the flour before measuring and resift it with the baking powder, cinnamon and salt. Cream the butter and gradually beat in the sugar until the mixture is soft and light. Add the egg, beating it in with the orange rind. Gradually add the sifted dry ingredients and stir in the bran. Fold in the nuts. Chill for about 1 hour.

Divide the chilled dough into 2 portions. Place a long piece of wax paper on the work surface and pat each half into a log about 1½ inches in diameter. Bring up the sides of the paper and press it against the dough. With your hands shape it into a symmetrical oval or round. Wrap in more wax paper or foil and place on a cookie sheet in the refrigerator or freezer to chill until it is very firm; this requires several hours in the refrigerator.

Preheat oven to 350°F., and adjust the racks to divide the oven into thirds. Butter 2 cookie sheets, or line them with foil. Unwrap the chilled logs. With a thin sharp knife, cut them into slices about ⅛ inch thick. Place rounds about 1 inch apart on the cookie sheets. Bake them for 8 to 10 minutes. After about 5 minutes, reverse the sheets from the upper to the lower racks and turn them from front to back. Cookies will be lightly colored. Cool them on a rack.

YIELD: 48 cookies

Walnut Crisps

These marvelous crisps can be made with other nuts such as almonds, black walnuts, filberts or pecans.

6 ounces shelled walnuts
¼ pound (1 stick) unsalted butter
1/3 cup granulated sugar

⅛ teaspoon salt, or less
1 teaspoon vanilla extract

Blanch the nuts and grind them very fine in a food processor or blender. Cream the butter with the sugar until light and fluffy. Stir in the ground nuts, salt and vanilla. Form the dough into a log about 1 inch in diameter. Wrap in wax paper and chill until firm, several hours or overnight.

Preheat oven to 350°F., and adjust a rack at the middle level. Line a cookie sheet with foil. Cut the chilled log into ⅛-inch slices and place them about 1 inch apart on the cookie sheet. If they do not all fit on one sheet, cut a second piece of foil the size of the sheet and place remaining slices on it. Bake for 6 to 8 minutes, or until cookies are lightly browned. Be careful as they burn easily. Remove them from the cookie sheet and place them on paper towels on a rack to cool. Slide the cookie sheet under the second sheet of foil. Allow a few minutes for the oven to return to the 350°F. level before placing it in the oven.

YIELD: 36 cookies

Almond Gingersnaps

The ginger makes a nice blend with the almonds in these Scandinavian cookies.

1¾ cups sifted all-purpose flour
½ teaspoon baking soda
Pinch of salt
2 teaspoons ground ginger
1 teaspoon ground cinnamon
1 teaspoon ground cloves

¼ pound (1 stick) unsalted butter
½ cup sugar
¼ cup honey or molasses
½ cup coarsely ground blanched
   almonds

Sift the flour before measuring and resift it with the baking soda, salt and spices. In a mixing bowl, cream the butter and sugar until fluffy. Beat in the honey or molasses. Stir in the flour and almonds and mix thoroughly. Turn out onto a lightly floured board and knead the dough until it is smooth. Place the dough on a piece of wax paper and form it into a round or oval log about 2 inches in diameter. Wrap in more wax paper or foil and chill for several hours, or until firm.

Preheat oven to 350°F., and adjust the racks to divide the oven into thirds. Slice the logs into ¼-inch-thick rounds, using a thin sharp knife. Place rounds on greased or foil-lined cookie sheets. Bake for 8 to 10 minutes, or until just golden. Remove from sheets and cool on racks.

YIELD: about 48 gingersnaps

Caraway Rounds

The English call these "seed biscuits"; some sources attribute their origin to the Romans.

2 cups sifted all-purpose flour	½ cup sugar
½ teaspoon baking soda	1 egg, lightly beaten
¼ teaspoon salt	2 teaspoons caraway seeds
¼ pound (1 stick) unsalted butter	2 to 3 Tablespoons milk

Sift the flour before measuring and resift it with the baking soda and salt. Cream the butter with the sugar until light. Beat in the egg and add the seeds. Gradually add the flour alternately with the milk until just mixed. Wrap dough in wax paper and chill. Or roll into a log about 2 inches in diameter and chill or freeze.

Roll out the dough on a lightly floured surface to ¼-inch thickness and cut out with a round cookie cutter. Or cut the log into ¼-inch-thick slices. Preheat oven to 400°F., and adjust the racks to divide the oven into thirds. Butter 2 cookie sheets, or line them with foil. Place the rounds 1 inch apart on the sheets. Bake the cookies for 8 to 10 minutes. After 5 or 6 minutes, reverse the cookie sheets from the upper to the lower rack and turn them from front to back. Cookies are done when they are light colored with a light brown edge. Transfer them to a rack to cool.

YIELD: about 48 rounds

Shrewsbury Cakes

These are known as Shrewsbury biscuits in England, where they originated. Delicately flavored, they are thin and crisp. They were meant to be served with tea or fruit. Some versions call for rosewater, others for rosewater and sherry, this one for rosewater and brandy.

2¼ cups sifted all-purpose flour	½ pound (2 sticks) unsalted butter
½ teaspoon ground nutmeg or mace	2/3 cup granulated sugar
½ teaspoon ground cinnamon	2 eggs
Pinch of salt	2 Tablespoons rosewater
	2 Tablespoons brandy

Sift the flour before measuring and resift it with the nutmeg or mace, cinnamon and salt. Cream the butter until soft. Beat in the sugar until light and fluffy. Add the eggs one at a time, beating after each addition. Stir in the rosewater and brandy and gradually add the sifted flour and spice mixture. Turn the dough out onto wax paper, wrap it well, and refrigerate for 2 hours, or overnight.

Preheat oven to 350°F., and adjust the racks to divide the oven into thirds. Roll out the dough to ⅛- or ¼-inch thickness and cut into rounds or other shapes, lightly flouring the cutter if necessary. Place 1 inch apart on ungreased or foil-lined baking sheets. Bake for 8 to 12 minutes, depending on thickness. About halfway through the baking time, reverse the cookie sheets from the upper to the lower rack and turn them from front to back. Cookies will be lightly colored.

YIELD: 40 rounds 2 inches across and ¼ inch thick, or 80 rounds 2 inches across and ⅛ inch thick

Caramel Nut Cookies

These are thick and soft with a moist chewy texture.

1¾ cups sifted all-purpose flour
1½ teaspoons baking soda
¼ teaspoon salt
¼ pound (1 stick) unsalted butter

1 cup firmly packed dark brown
  sugar
1 egg
½ cup finely chopped nuts

Preheat oven to 400°F., and adjust the racks to divide the oven into thirds. Line 2 cookie sheets with foil, or leave them plain. Sift the flour before measuring and resift it with the baking soda and salt. Cream the butter until soft. Beat in the sugar until light and fluffy. Add the egg, beating it in, and gradually add the sifted flour mixture. Mix in the chopped nuts. Roll the dough out on a floured pastry cloth or between 2 sheets of wax paper to ⅜-inch thickness. Cut into rounds or other shapes. Place the cut-outs about 1 inch apart on the cookie sheets.

Bake for 8 to 10 minutes, or until lightly browned. After about 6 minutes, reverse the cookie sheets from the upper to the lower racks and turn them from front to back at the same time. Transfer to a rack to cool.

YIELD: 40 cookies
VARIATION: Form into a log, chill, and slice for baking.

White Sugar Cookies

These cookies come out of the oven almost white. They make a nice background for decorating with colored sugar.

2½ cups sifted all-purpose flour
½ pound (2 sticks) unsalted butter
1 cup sifted confectioners' sugar

1 Tablespoon milk
1 teaspoon vanilla extract

Preheat oven to 325°F., and adjust the racks to divide the oven into thirds. Butter 2 cookie sheets, or line them with foil. Sift the flour before measuring. Cream the butter until soft. Gradually add the sugar and beat until the mixture is very fluffy. Add the flour gradually until it is barely incorported. Add the milk and vanilla. Turn the dough out on a lightly floured surface and knead it briefly. Roll the dough out on a floured pastry cloth or between 2 sheets of wax paper to ¼-inch thickness. Cut out rounds or other shapes and place them about 1 inch apart on the cookie sheets.

Bake the cookies for 18 to 22 minutes. After about 12 minutes, reverse the sheets from the upper to the lower racks and turn them front to back. The cookies barely color. Transfer to a rack to cool.

YIELD: about 48 cookies
VARIATION: The dough can be formed into long rounds to be chilled thoroughly and sliced for baking.

Empire Biscuits

An old Virginia recipe that is believed to go back to Colonial times. It consists of two cookies sandwiched together with currant jelly and topped with a white glaze icing.

1¼ cups sifted all-purpose flour	Currant jelly
¼ teaspoon ground mace	2 teaspoons water
¼ teaspoon ground cinnamon	½ cup confectioners' sugar
¼ pound (1 stick) unsalted butter	Glacé red cherries (optional), cut
¼ cup granulated sugar	into bits

Sift the flour before measuring and resift it with the mace and cinnamon. Cream the butter with the sugar until soft and creamy. Gradually add the flour, blending it in completely. Chill the dough for about 1 hour, or until stiff enough to handle.

Preheat oven to 400°F., and adjust the racks to divide the oven into thirds. Line 2 baking sheets with foil, or butter them lightly. Roll out the dough as thin as possible (less than ⅛ inch) and cut into 1½-inch rounds. Transfer these rounds to the prepared baking sheets.

Bake from 4 to 6 minutes, or until lightly browned around the edges. If necessary, reverse the baking sheets from the upper to the lower racks and turn them from front to back to ensure even browning. The cookies take slightly longer if they are ⅛ inch or more in thickness. When cookies are done, transfer them to a wire rack to cool. Put 2 cookies together, bottom sides facing each other, with a thin layer of currant jelly between them. Ice them with a glaze made up of the water and confectioners' sugar, and decorate them with bits of cherries.

YIELD: 24 double cookies

South Dakota Almond Cookies

These are large, crisp, spicy and very sweet. My friend Maxine tells me this has been a traditional holiday treat in her family for several generations.

2¼ cups sifted all-purpose flour
2 teaspoons baking powder
1 scant teaspoon gound allspice
1 scant teaspoon ground cinnamon
¼ teaspoon ground cloves

1 pound dark brown sugar (see Note)
2 ounces (½ stick) unsalted butter
3 eggs
4 ounces blanched almonds, finely ground (1 cup)

Sift the flour before measuring it and resift it with the baking powder and the spices. Sift the brown sugar. Cream the butter with sugar. Add the eggs one at a time, beating after each addition. Beat in the almonds. Add the sifted dry ingredients, blending them in. Line an empty wax-paper or foil box, 12 inches long and 2 inches square, with a large sheet of wax paper. Scrape the dough out of the mixing bowl and spread it evenly in the paper-lined box. Chill or freeze it until firm enough to slice.

Preheat oven to 375°F., and adjust the rack to divide the oven into thirds. Butter 2 cookie sheets, or line them with foil. With a thin, sharp knife, cut the dough into slices ¼ inch thick. Place slices 2 inches apart on the cookie sheets. These will spread during baking. Bake for 15 to 18 minutes, or until lightly browned. After 8 or 9 minutes, reverse the cookie sheets from the upper to the lower rack and turn them from front to back. Transfer to a rack to cool.

YIELD: 48 squares, 3-inch size
VARIATION: Rather than chilling and slicing the dough, drop it by teaspoons onto the cookie sheets, to make about 48 rounds.
NOTE: I think these cookies are much too sweet but most people love them. I think 2 cups of sugar is sufficient.

Black Pepper Cookies

These have a nice spicy bite to them. Try the chocolate variation, too.

1½ cups sifted all-purpose flour
1 teaspoon baking powder
¼ teaspoon salt
1½ teaspoons ground ginger
1 teaspoon ground cinnamon
¼ teaspoon ground cloves

½ teaspoon black pepper
¼ pound (1 stick) unsalted butter
1 cup sugar
1 egg
½ teaspoon vanilla extract

Sift the flour before measuring and resift it with the baking powder, salt and spices. Cream the butter with the sugar until light and fluffy. Beat in the egg and the vanilla. Gradually add the sifted dry ingredients, beating them in until just incorporated. Wrap the dough and chill it overnight.

Preheat oven to 375°F., and adjust the racks to divide the oven into thirds. Butter 2 cookie sheets, or line them with foil. Working with half of the dough at a time, roll it out on a lightly floured pastry cloth, or between 2 sheets of wax paper, to ⅛-inch thickness. Cut into shapes with a cookie cutter. Place cookies 1 inch apart on the prepared sheets. Bake for 8 to 10 minutes, or until lightly browned. After about 5 minutes, reverse the sheets from the upper to the lower racks and turn them from front to back. Transfer the cookies to a rack to cool.

YIELD: 30 cookies
VARIATION: Omit the ginger. Sift 2/3 cup cocoa powder with the flour and increase the butter to 6 ounces (1½ sticks). This makes 36 cookies.

Mint Treasures

These really do surprise people. A thin mint candy is enclosed in cookie dough and baked. Don't try these on a hot day!

2 cups sifted all-purpose flour
¼ teaspoon salt
1 teaspoon baking powder
¼ pound (1 stick) unsalted butter
1 cup granulated sugar, *or*
  ½ cup granulated sugar and
  ½ cup firmly packed brown sugar

1 egg
3 Tablespoons light cream or milk
½ teaspoon vanilla extract
30 very thin chocolate covered mints, preferably square
30 pecan or walnut halves

Sift the flour before measuring and resift it with the salt and baking powder. Cream the butter until soft. Beat in the sugar, or sugars, until light and fluffy. Beat in the egg and the cream or milk. Stir in the vanilla and gradually add the sifted dry ingredients, beating until blended. Wrap the dough in wax paper and chill it for several hours or overnight. The dough must be very firm for rolling.

Preheat oven to 375°F., and adjust the racks to divide the oven into thirds. Butter and flour 2 cookie sheets, or line them with foil. Working with about half of the dough and keeping the rest refrigerated, roll the dough out very thin, about ⅛ inch thick. Measure the mints and cut rectangles of dough slightly more than twice the size of the mint. For a 1-inch mint cut a rectange 1¼ x 2½ inches. Place the mint on one half of the rectangle, fold over the other half to encase it, and crimp the edges with the tines of a fork to enclose the mint. Place a nut half on top of each, in the center. If the kitchen is warm, refrigerate them as you go, on a cookie sheet.

Bake for 10 to 12 minutes, or until lightly browned. After 6 or 7 minutes, reverse the cookie sheets from the upper to the lower rack and turn them from front to back. Let stand on the foil liner, or the cookie sheet, for a minute or so before transferring them to a rack to cool.

YIELD: 30 cookies

Orange Continentals

These delectably rich cookies are made with a dough that uses hard-cooked egg yolks, an ingredient called for in many European recipes.

2 cups sifted all-purpose flour
½ teaspoon salt
½ pound (2 sticks) unsalted
  butter
¾ cup sugar

5 hard-cooked egg yolks
1 teaspoon vanilla or orange extract,
  or 2 teaspoons Grand Marnier
  liqueur
2 teaspoons grated orange rind

Sift the flour before measuring and resift it with the salt. Cream the butter until soft. Beat in the sugar until light and fluffy. Sieve in the hard-cooked yolks and beat in the vanilla or orange extract or liqueur, and the orange rind. Gradually stir in the sifted flour and salt. Wrap the dough in wax paper or foil and chill for at least 1 hour, or until firm enough to roll out for cutting. Or form it into a log to slice it into rounds after chilling; however, I feel that this dough deserves a little more elegant treatment.

Preheat oven to 350°F., and adjust the racks to divide the oven into thirds. Butter 2 cookie sheets, or line them with foil. Roll out the cookie dough on a floured pastry cloth or between 2 sheets of wax paper to ¼-inch thickness. Using cutters, cut the dough into small crescents, rounds, stars, or other fancy shapes. Place them about ½ inch apart on the prepared cookie sheets. See Variations for suggested toppings. However, they are delicious plain.

Bake for 12 to 15 minutes, or until lightly browned. After about 8 minutes, reverse the cookie sheets from the upper to the lower racks and turn them from front to back. Transfer to a rack to cool.

YIELD: 48 cookies

VARIATION:

1. Before baking, brush the tops of the cookies with ¼ cup heavy cream. Combine ½ cup granulated sugar and ½ cup ground nuts and sprinkle on the cookies.

2. Eliminate the orange extract and orange rind and substitute 1 teaspoon vanilla extract. Before baking, brush the tops of the cookies with 1 egg beaten with 1 teaspoon milk. Sprinkle on the cookies finely chopped nuts or cinnamon sugar (see p. 24) or poppy seeds.

Shortenin' Bread

For all the little babies who "love shortenin' bread," here is a fairly typical version.

2 cups sifted all-purpose flour
¼ teaspoon salt
¼ teaspoon baking powder
¼ teaspoon ground nutmeg

½ pound (2 sticks) unsalted butter
1 cup firmly packed dark brown sugar

Preheat oven to 325°F., and place a rack at the middle level. Sift the flour before measuring and resift it with the salt, baking powder and nutmeg. Cream the butter until soft. Beat in the sugar until creamy and light. Gradually add the sifted dry ingredients. Press the dough lightly into an ungreased pan 6 x 12 inches, or in a rectangle that size on an ungreased cookie sheet. The dough should be 1/3 inch thick. With a pastry wheel, lightly mark off 1½-inch squares, cutting only partway through.

Bake for 35 to 40 minutes, until dried out and only slightly colored. Let cool before breaking off the squares.

YIELD: 32 squares

Sandwich Cookies

These are very festive and impressive. They can be made by sandwiching two rounds together with a filling between, or the filling can be placed on half of the cookie and the other half folded over. The variation sandwiches them after baking.

The filling can be a simple one such as apple, peach or prune butter, or the sweeter one given here. Make filling while the dough is chilling.

2½ cups sifted all-purpose flour
1 teaspoon baking powder
½ teaspoon salt
6 ounces (1½ sticks) unsalted butter

½ to 2/3 cup granulated sugar (depending on filling)
2 eggs
1 teaspoon vanilla extract
1 cup Dried-Fruit Filling (recipe follows)

Sift the flour before measuring and resift it with the baking powder and salt. Cream the butter with the sugar until light and fluffy. Use ½ cup sugar if you prepare Dried-Fruit filling; use 2/3 cup sugar for plain fruit butter. Add the eggs, beating after each addition, and stir in the vanilla. Wrap the dough and chill it for several hours or overnight.

Preheat oven to 375°F., and adjust the racks to divide the oven into thirds. Butter 2 cookie sheets, or line them with foil. Work with about one third of the dough at a time, leaving the rest refrigerated. Roll the dough out on a lightly floured board or floured pastry cloth, or between 2 sheets of wax paper, to ⅛-inch thickness. Cut into 3-inch rounds with a lightly floured cutter. Spread about 1 teaspoon of filling on one round, top it with another round, and crimp the edges slightly with a fork to seal, if necessary.

Bake for 9 to 12 minutes, until lightly browned. After 6 or 7 minutes, reverse the sheets from the upper to the lower rack and turn them from front to back. Transfer to a rack to cool.

YIELD: 36 cookies

Dried-Fruit Filling

1 cup chopped dried apricots,
  dates or figs
6 Tablespoons granulated sugar
5 Tablespoons boiling water

½ teaspoon grated lemon rind
1 teaspoon lemon juice
2 teaspoons butter
Pinch of salt

Combine all the ingredients in a saucepan and bring to a boil, stirring, until the mixture is thick. Allow filling to cool to room temperature.

VARIATION: Cut the dough into rounds and cut out the centers of half of the rounds. The cut-out centers can be baked as small cookies or rerolled. Bake the cookies for 7 to 10 minutes. After about 5 minutes, reverse the cookie sheets. Transfer to a rack to cool. Spread thick raspberry or apricot jam on the solid rounds. Top them with the cut-out rounds and add a bit more jam to the center holes.

Sand Tarts

A real classic whose name originated with the coarse sugar that was sprinkled on the top. The present-day sugar is not as coarse but cinnamon and sugar, or ground nuts, add the sandy texture. You can sprinkle the cookies with crystal sugar, or pound lumps of sugar to a grainy consistency.

2 cups sifted all-purpose flour *or* cake flour (see Note)
¼ pound (1 stick) unsalted butter
1 cup granulated sugar
1 egg

½ teaspoon vanilla extract (optional)
1 egg white, beaten lightly
Cinnamon sugar or coarse sugar
Walnuts or almonds (optional) for tops of cookies

Sift the flour before measuring and set it aside. Cream the butter until soft. Beat in the sugar until light and fluffy. Beat in the egg and the vanilla if you use it. Gradually add the sifted flour, beating it in until well blended. Refrigerate the dough for several hours, or overnight.

Preheat oven to 375°F., and adjust the racks to divide the oven into thirds. Butter 2 cookie sheets, or line them with foil. Roll the dough out on a floured pastry cloth or between 2 sheets of wax paper to ⅛-inch thickness. Cut into shapes with a cookie cutter and place them about ½ inch apart on the cookie sheets. Brush the tops with egg white and sprinkle on a little cinnamon sugar or coarse (crystal) sugar. Top with nut halves or a few chopped nuts, if desired.

Bake for 8 to 10 minutes, until the edges are a deep golden color. After about 5 minutes, reverse the sheets from the upper to the lower racks and turn them from front to back. Let cool on the cookie sheets for a few minutes before transferring to a rack to cool.

YIELD: 50 cookies

VARIATION:

1. Use almond extract in place of vanilla and top each cookie with a whole blanched almond.

2. Add 1 cup chopped nuts to the batter.

3. Form into a log and slice thin, rather than rolling and cutting out. Dough freezes well.

4. Substitute light brown sugar for granulated sugar.

NOTE: The use of cake flour produces a cookie with a very delicate texture; try it. However, all-purpose flour works fine.

Purists decry the use of vanilla and consider it a modern addition.

Gerta's Small Yeast Cookies

Another delicious sweet from my friend, Gerta Kessler. Do try her Raisin Squares, also (p. 160). These yeast cookies need an overnight rest, so plan accordingly. They freeze beautifully, too.

1 envelope active dry yeast, or 1 cake compressed fresh yeast
¼ cup warm milk or water (105° to 115° F. for dry yeast, 80° to 90° F. for fresh yeast)
½ teaspoon granulated sugar
2½ cups sifted all-purpose flour
½ pound (2 sticks) unsalted butter cut into bits

Meringue Topping

3 egg whites
¼ teaspoon cream of tartar
½ teaspoon ground cinnamon
¾ cup granulated sugar
½ cup raisins
½ cup chopped nuts (optional)

Dissolve the yeast in the warm milk or water with the ½ teaspoon sugar. Let this sit for about 5 minutes; by that time the liquid should have a high foamy "head." This is known as "proofing" the yeast, to ensure that it is alive and active. Sift the flour before measuring and combine it with the butter. Add the liquid yeast mixture, kneading lightly. Form the mixture into a ball, wrap in plastic or foil, and refrigerate it overnight.

Next day, preheat oven to 350°F., and adjust the racks to divide the oven into thirds. Butter 2 baking sheets, or line them with foil.

Remove the dough from the refrigerator. Place the egg whites in a mixing bowl. If they are cold, set the bowl over warm water and stir them lightly until they are at room temperature. Beat the whites, adding the cream of tartar, until soft peaks form. Stir the cinnamon into the granulated sugar and gradually add this to the egg whites, beating until the whites form stiff peaks.

Divide the dough into 4 parts. Roll each piece out on a floured surface, or between 2 sheets of wax paper, into a rectangle about 6 x 9 inches and ¼ inch thick. Spread the rectangle with one fourth of the meringue and sprinkle with one fourth of the raisins and nuts. Roll the dough up like a jelly roll and cut it into ½-inch slices. Place the slices on the prepared baking sheet. Repeat with the balance of the dough.

Bake for about 15 minutes. After about 10 minutes, reverse the cookie sheets from the upper to the lower rack and turn them from front to back. They are done when lightly browned. Transfer to a rack to cool.

YIELD: 72 cookies

NOTE: Gerta freezes hers by placing them in a plastic shoe box. She lays them flat and is careful not to crowd them. She separates the cookies with foil between the layers. They keep very well and defrost quickly.

Castine Raisin Cookies

This great old recipe was given to my friend Libby by a lady named Barbara Perkins who comes from that wonderful Maine town on Castine Bay.

2½ cups sifted all-purpose flour
¼ teaspoon salt
½ teaspoon baking soda *and*
  1 teaspoon cream of tartar, *or*
  2 teaspoons baking powder
¼ pound (1 stick) unsalted butter

1 cup granulated sugar
1 egg
½ cup milk
1 teaspoon vanilla extract
Raisin Filling (recipe follows)

Sift the flour before measuring and resift it with the salt and with the mixture of baking soda and cream of tartar or baking powder above. Cream the butter until soft. Beat in the sugar until light and fluffy. Add the egg, beating it in well, and the milk. Stir in the vanilla and gradually add the sifted dry ingredients. Chill the dough for several hours, or overnight.

Preheat oven to 375°F., and adjust the racks to divide the oven into thirds. Butter 2 cookie sheets or 1 large sheet 14 x 17 inches, or line them with foil. If you use the single large sheet, bake it on the upper level of the oven. Roll the dough out between 2 sheets of wax paper or on a floured pastry cloth to ⅛-inch thickness. Cut the dough into 3-inch rounds. Half of them may be cut with a doughnut cutter so that the filling shows through the round hole. Place a rounded teaspoon of the filling on one of the rounds. Cover it with another round. Using a floured fork, press the edges of the cookies with the tines to hold the filling in. Transfer to the prepared cookie sheets.

Bake for about 12 minutes, until lightly colored. If necessary for even browning, after about 8 minutes, reverse the sheets from the upper to the lower rack and turn them from front to back. Transfer to a rack to cool.

YIELD: 20 cookies

Raisin Filling

1 cup raisins
1/3 cup granulated sugar
1/3 cup hot water

1 Tablespoon flour
2 teaspoons unsalted butter
¼ teaspoon vanilla extract

Combine all ingredients in a heavy saucepan. Bring the mixture to a boil, stirring, and continue to stir until it thickens. Remove from heat and cool.

VARIATIONS: Place a scant teaspoon of the filling on half of a round and fold over the other half to make half-moons. Crimp the outside edges with a fork to seal in the filling.

Add ½ teaspoon grated lemon rind and 2 teaspoons lemon juice to the filling.

Scotch Shortbread

One of the more delightful parts of writing this book was sampling all the various shortbreads — all "authentic" recipes, of course. There is one I only heard about which is a "secret" recipe and calls for an unspecified amount of fine semolina. To my surprise, a bit of research revealed that for generations, the Scottish pastry makers were traditionally Italian.

Shortbread is often formed in conventional cookie cutter shapes. However, there is also the version known as "Petticoat Tails" (which is imported in tins from Scotland). This is a round, usually 7 inches in diameter, which is marked off in pie-shaped wedges. The wedges do not come to the conventional point in the center because there is another small circle marked off there. "Petticoat Tails" are supposedly named thus because the wedges, with the slightly rounded tip, resemble the pattern pieces of a petticoat. I came across another explanation for the name, but am unable to substantiate it. Supposedly, when Mary Stuart, Queen of Scotland, returned there from France, her ladies-in-waiting brought with them a recipe for petits gâteaux tarles, *a name that became corrupted to "petticoat tails."*

Some recipes use only flour, others use part rice flour, and some use cornstarch, which the English call corn flour. One could spend years tracking down all the variations. Most recipes agree on the basic quantities of butter and flour but differ in amount and type of sugar; some call for confectioners' sugar, others for granulated, and some for brown sugar (see Shortenin' Bread as well as Variations). This is the recipe I like.

2 cups sifted all-purpose flour ½ pound (2 sticks) unsalted butter

¼ cup confectioners' sugar
¼ cup sweet rice flour (see Note)

Preheat oven to 300°F., and place rack at the middle level. Sift the all-purpose flour before measuring and set it aside. Cream the butter until very soft and light. Sift the confectioners' sugar with the rice flour and beat this into the butter. Work the sifted flour in, kneading until the mixture is smooth. Roll out or pat out to ¼- or 1/3-inch thickness. Using cookie cutters, make various shapes such as rounds, squares, diamonds, etc. Place pieces close to, but not touching, each other on ungreased baking sheets.

Bake for 50 to 60 minutes, or until barely colored. Only the edges should be slightly sand colored. Transfer to a rack to cool.

To form squares, pat the dough into an ungreased pan 9 x 9 x 2 inches or 7 x 11 inches. Mark the dough lightly with a pastry wheel, but do not cut through.

To form Petticoat Tails press the dough out on 2 ungreased rounds 8 inches in diameter. Use inverted cake pans or the inserts of quiche pans. Mark a 2-inch round in the center and then mark off the outer portion into 8 or more pie-shaped wedges. Do not cut through the dough. Flute or crimp the edges and lightly prick the surface.

YIELD: approximately 45 small cookies

VARIATIONS: I was given many recipes for shortbread, each of which was reputedly the authentic version. I have decided that there is no one authentic version and for those of you who might want to devote a great deal of time to shortbread making, I am listing herewith some of the others:

1. 2 cups sifted all-purpose flour
    ½ pound (2 sticks) unsalted butter
    ¾ cup confectioners' sugar

2. Same as above but with ½ cup of granulated or light brown sugar instead of confectioners' sugar.

3. 1½ cups sifted all-purpose flour
    1½ cups rice flour
    ½ pound (2 sticks) unsalted butter
    1 cup granulated sugar

4. Same as number 3 with cornstarch substituted for rice flour.

5. 1 pound sifted all-purpose flour (3¾ cups)
    ¾ pound rice flour
    1 pound unsalted butter
    ½ pound granulated sugar
    ½ teaspoon salt

6. And here, from another Scottish lady, still another version which calls for:

1 pound (4 sticks) unsalted butter
½ cup confectioners' sugar
½ cup light brown sugar
1 egg
7 cups sifted all-purpose flour

7. Finally, a version called Irish Shortbread which uses 2 cups flour and ½ pound butter, ½ cup brown sugar, 1½ teaspoons cream and ¾ teaspoon ground ginger.

NOTE: The rice flour is not essential, but it makes the texture softer and more crumbly. This is not brown rice flour. It is sometimes called "sweet rice flour" and is available at health-food stores. Try making one batch without and *try* to decide which you prefer. A British friend of mine tried to help me decide one afternoon; when both batches were gone, we still hadn't decided.

Pastry-Bag Cookies,
Meringues and Macaroons

Cats' Tongues

In France, where these originated they are, of course, called langues de chats. *As with most classic recipes, there are different versions with different amounts of ingredients.*

¼ pound (1 stick) unsalted butter
½ cup granulated sugar
⅛ teaspoon vanilla extract

2 egg whites
1/3 cup *unsifted* all-purpose flour

Preheat oven to 400°F., and adjust the racks to divide the oven into thirds. Butter and flour 2 baking sheets. Cream the butter until very soft and fluffy. Add the sugar gradually and beat in the vanilla. The mixture should be very light and soft. Beat the egg whites briefly with a fork. Add about 1 tablespoon of the whites at a time to the butter, folding them in quickly and lightly with a rubber spatula. Don't try to mix them in completely. Sift about one fourth of the flour over the batter and quickly cut it in with the spatula, repeating until all the flour has been just cut in. Fit a pastry bag with a plain tube about ⅜ inch in diameter (#4) and fill it about two thirds full. Pipe the batter onto the prepared baking sheets in strips 3 inches long and the thickness of a finger. Leave about 3 inches of space between them because they spread a lot.

Bake the cookies for 8 to 10 minutes, or until the edges have browned. Check the oven after about 6 minutes but do not reverse the sheets unless they are browning very unevenly.

YIELD: about 36 cookies
VARIATION: In place of the vanilla extract, add 1 teaspoon lemon juice and the grated rind of 1 lemon. Pipe rounds of batter about 2 inches apart. They are done when the edges are browned.

Ladyfingers

A light dry French classic, good on its own or sandwiched with jam between. It is also the basis for many molded desserts (Charlotte Russe, etc.). Tuck some of these in the freezer for a special dessert.

3 whole eggs, separated
1 extra egg white
2/3 cup sifted confectioners' sugar
1 teaspoon vanilla extract

Pinch of salt
2/3 cup sifted cake flour
1 cup (approximately) confectioners' sugar, in a sieve or shaker

Preheat oven to 300°F., and adjust the racks to the upper and middle levels. Butter and flour 2 baking sheets; knock off the excess flour. (A foil liner does not work with these.) Fit a pastry bag with a plain tube ½ inch in diameter. Separate the eggs, dropping the yolks into a mixing bowl and the whites, plus the extra white, into a second bowl. Sift the confectioners' sugar before measuring it. (If you have previously sifted it, there is no need to resift.) Sift the flour before measuring and return the measured flour to the sifter, set on a piece of wax paper. Beat the egg yolks until they are thick. Gradually add 1/3 cup of the confectioners' sugar, beating until thick and lemon-colored. Beat in the vanilla. Start beating the egg whites, add the pinch of salt, and continue beating until soft peaks form. Gradually add the remaining 1/3 cup confectioners' sugar and beat until stiff peaks are formed. Fold about one fourth of the egg whites into the yolks and sift about one fourth of the flour onto the mixture. Fold the flour in very lightly so as not to deflate the batter and don't try to incorporate every last bit of the flour. Continue folding in the whites and the flour in 3 more additions. Scoop the batter into the pastry bag. Squeeze out the ladyfingers approximately 4 inches long and 1½ inches wide, about 1½ inches apart. Sprinkle the fingers with confectioners' sugar, covering them thoroughly.

Bake for about 20 minutes, or until the fingers are a very pale beige with a slight crust. Remove them immediately from the baking sheets and cool them on a rack. They will keep in an airtight container for about 10 days. They freeze very well.

YIELD: 24 to 30 ladyfingers   (Much depends on the weather; see Eggs, p. 16.)

VARIATION: Mrs. Beeton calls her "ladies fingers" Savoy biscuits and uses the grated rind of a lemon in place of vanilla. It makes a nice variation.

NOTE: Lacking a pastry bag, you can shape the fingers using 2 tablespoons of batter. Using a rubber spatula and a spoon, spread 1 tablespoon in a line 4 inches long and ¾ inch wide. Place the second tablespoon parallel to, and touching, the first one.

Meringue Kisses

These are fun to make and have lots of variations. Since they have no butter or flour, their calorie count is fairly low.

4 egg whites, at room temperature
Pinch of salt
¼ teaspoon cream of tartar
1 cup granulated sugar

1 teaspoon vanilla extract *or* ½ teaspoon grated lemon rind and ½ teaspoon vanilla extract

Preheat oven to 250°F., and adjust the racks to divide the oven into thirds. Line 2 baking sheets with foil; you can butter and flour them but foil is preferable. Start beating the egg whites with an electric beater or mixer, or manually with a balloon whisk or rotary egg beater. Add the salt and the cream of tartar and continue beating until soft peaks form. Gradually add the sugar, about 1 tablespoon at a time, beating all the while, until the whites form stiff and shiny peaks. Add the vanilla toward the end of the beating. With a teaspoon and a rubber spatula, or 2 spoons, place rounded teaspoons of the meringue about 2 inches apart on the cookie sheets. Round the tops or leave them peaked, as you prefer. If you prefer, form them with a pastry bag fitted with a plain or star-shaped tip, making rounds about 1½ inches in diameter.

Bake for 35 to 45 minutes, until the meringues are firm and creamy colored. If you want somewhat chewy meringues, remove the foil liner with the kisses and place it on a rack to cool. When cool, peel the foil from the kisses, using a spatula. It should be possible to remove meringues from floured cookie sheets without a spatula. Transfer the kisses to a rack to cool. If you want crisper meringues, turn off the oven when they are done and leave them in the closed oven for 2 to 3 hours. Do not open the oven door. You can leave them overnight, if you like.

YIELD: 40 meringues

VARIATIONS:

CHOCOLATE KISSES: (sometimes known as Nun's Puffs) At the end of the beating, grate 1 ounce (1 square) unsweetened chocolate into the meringue mixture.

NUT KISSES: At the end of the beating, fold in 1 cup finely chopped blanched almonds, pistachios, walnuts, pecans, etc.

COCONUT KISSES: At the end of the beating, fold in 1½ cups flaked or shredded coconut.

ORANGE KISSES: At the end of the beating, substitute 1 teaspoon orange extract for the vanilla; fold in 1 tablespoon grated orange rind.

Strawberry Meringues

These are light and sweet, with a delicate rose color. Wrapped airtight, they will keep in the freezer for months after baking. Although they could be dropped from a spoon, they are much more impressive when piped through a pastry bag.

These are most easily prepared with an electric mixer. Lacking one, you will find another pair of hands helpful. You will find a candy thermometer useful.

1 package (10 oz.) frozen strawberries
1 cup granulated sugar

4 egg whites, at room temperature
¼ tsp. cream of tartar

Preheat oven to 225°F., and adjust the racks to divide the oven into thirds. Butter and flour 2 cookie sheets, shaking off excess flour, or line them with foil. Drain the thawed strawberries over a bowl and pour the juice into a small heavy saucepan. The pan should be a narrow one or the candy thermometer will be touching the bottom of the pan and will not be accurate. Add the sugar to the juice and set the pan over low heat. Purée the strawberries in a blender or food processor and place them in a small bowl. Put the egg whites in the clean, dry bowl of an electric mixer or in a clean, dry metal bowl, preferably copper. Stir the strawberry juice and sugar only until the sugar is dissolved. Without stirring, continue to cook the syrup until it reaches 240° F. on a candy thermometer (soft-ball stage). Lacking a thermometer, drop a small amount into ice water where it should form a soft ball. Stir puréed strawberries into the syrup and continue cooking over very low heat for a few minutes. Then turn off heat.

Beat the egg whites until they are foamy. Add the cream of tartar and continue beating until the whites form stiff peaks. Slowly pour the hot strawberry syrup into the whites while continuing to beat them. The syrup must be added slowly, in a thin stream, while beating the whites constantly. Beat until the whites become cool again. They will be very stiff, shiny and rose colored. Half-fill a pastry bag fitted with a star-tube, and pipe out rosettes, or use a ribbon tube for fingers or diamonds. Or press a heart-shaped cookie cutter into the floured cookie sheet to make an outline that can be followed for heart shapes. To expand the meringues into a dessert, make rounds or ovals with walls; you will then have a shell that can be filled with fruit or ice cream.

Place the filled cookie sheets in the oven and reduce the temperature to 200°F. Bake meringues for about 1 hour. After about 30 minutes, reverse the sheets from upper to lower racks and turn them from front to back. The meringues will not change color or shape; they just dry out. They are done when you can gently loosen them from the cookie sheet. While they are warm they are faintly pliable. As they cool, they become crisp and fragile. Loosen them all but leave them on the sheets until they are cool.

YIELD: About 48 rounds or hearts, 2-inch size
VARIATION: If using fresh strawberries, the proportions would be: 1 cup sugar and 1/3 cup water for the syrup. You would need about 1 pint of strawberries (¾ cup puréed).

If substituting blueberries (blue meringues!) strain out the skins.

Meringue Surprises

Both chocolate and nuts are tucked away in these.

2 egg whites, at room temperature
⅛ teaspoon salt
⅛ teaspoon cream of tartar
1 teaspoon vanilla extract

¾ cup granulated sugar
6 ounces semisweet chocolate bits
¼ cup chopped nuts (walnuts, pecans, black walnuts, etc.)

Preheat oven to 300°F., and adjust the racks to divide the oven into thirds. Butter and flour 2 cookie sheets, shaking off excess flour, or line the sheets with foil. Beat the egg whites briefly before adding the salt and cream of tartar. Continue beating until the whites are stiff but not dry. Add the vanilla and gradually beat in the sugar, continuing to beat. The whites should form stiff peaks when all the sugar has been added. Fold in the chocolate bits and chopped nuts. Using a spoon and a rubber spatula, gently drop the meringues by the teaspoon onto the prepared sheets.

Bake for about 25 minutes. Meringues will be soft to the touch but they become crisper as they cool. Loosen them on the cookie sheets but do not remove them until completely cooled.

YIELD: 24 meringues

Hornets' Nests

Don't let the name put you off. These are wonderful.

¾ cup chopped almonds
1 Tablespoon plus 2/3 cup granulated sugar
2 egg whites, at room temperature

½ teaspoon cream of tartar
Pinch of salt
6 Tablespoons unsweetened cocoa powder

Preheat oven to 300°F., and adjust the racks to divide the oven into thirds. Butter and flour 2 cookie sheets, shaking off excess flour. In a heavy skillet, lightly brown the almonds with the tablespoon of sugar over medium heat. Stir constantly to prevent the sugar burning. When the almonds are toasted light brown, remove them from the pan and spread them on a plate or sheet of wax paper or foil. Beat the egg whites until foamy. Add the cream of tartar and salt and continue to beat until soft peaks form. Start slowly adding the sugar while still beating. Add the cocoa and beat until the whites are stiff but not dry. Quickly fold in the almonds. Using a teaspoon and a rubber spatula, drop mounds of the meringue on the prepared baking sheets, flattening them or leaving them peaked.

Bake for 20 to 25 minutes, being careful not to overbake, until meringues are partly dry and will retain their shape. Cool on a rack before storing in an airtight container. They will keep for about 4 weeks.

YIELD: about 36 meringues

Meringue Nut Bars

A delicious way to use up extra egg whites. These are easy to make; they need only egg whites, sugar, nuts and flavoring.

3 egg whites, at room temperature
¼ teaspoon cream of tartar
1 cup granulated sugar
1 teaspoon grated orange or lemon rind *or* 1 teaspoon vanilla extract

1 pound shelled pecans, walnuts, filberts, etc., finely chopped (4 cups)

Preheat oven to 325°F., and adjust the racks to divide the oven into thirds. Butter and flour 2 cookie sheets and shake off the excess flour, or line them with foil. Beat the egg whites lightly, add the cream of tartar, and continue to beat until they start to form soft peaks. Gradually add the sugar, about 1 tablespoon at a time. Continue beating, while adding all the sugar, until the whites are stiff and shiny. Carefully remove a generous cup of the meringue and set it aside. Fold the grated rind or vanilla and the nuts into the remaining whites.

On a floured work surface, or between 2 sheets of wax paper, roll out half of the nut and meringue mixture about ¼ inch thick. Roll it into a rectangle approximately 9 by 12 inches. Spread half of the reserved plain meringue on the top. Warm a thin sharp knife under hot water, dry it, and flour it lightly. Cut the rolled-out meringue mixture into bars 1½ x 3 inches. Place bars 1 inch apart on the prepared cookie sheet. Repeat the rolling and cutting procedure with the remaining meringue. Bake for about 25 minutes, or until the topping is firm and creamy looking. Transfer to a rack to cool.

YIELD: **48 bars**

Chocolate Almond Meringue Bars

This recipe makes a fairly large batch, which is fortunate as they vanish before your eyes.

2 ounces (2 squares) unsweetened chocolate, melted and cooled, *or* 6 Tablespoons unsweetened cocoa powder

3 egg whites, at room temperature

⅛ teaspoon cream of tarter

6 Tablespoons granulated sugar

4 ounces blanched almonds, coarsely ground or shredded (1 cup)

½ teaspoon vanilla extract

Preheat oven to 325°F., and place a rack at the middle level. Butter a pan 9 x 13 inches. If you are using chocolate, melt it and set aside to cool. Beat the egg whites slightly, add cream of tartar, and beat until the whites form soft peaks. Gradually, and very slowly, add the sugar, beating the whites constantly. Fold in the melted chocolate or the cocoa and ½ cup of the almonds. Gently stir in the vanilla. Lightly spread the mixture in the prepared pan, making an even layer. Sprinkle remaining almonds on top.

Bake for about 45 minutes, until the meringue dries out a bit and becomes firm. Allow the meringue to cool in the pan. With a hot knife, cut meringue lengthwise to make 9 long strips. Cut the strips crosswise into 2-inch lengths.

YIELD: 54 bars, 1 x 2 inches

Macaroons

These are Italian in origin, although they have become a French favorite. It is believed that the name comes from the Italian "maccare," meaning to crush or mash (also believed to be the root of the word macaroni).

½ pound almonds, blanched and well dried
¾ cup granulated sugar
3 or 4 egg whites (½ cup)

¼ teaspoon cream of tartar
Pinch of salt
½ teaspoon almond extract
Confectioners' sugar (optional)

Preheat oven to 350°F., and adjust the racks to divide the oven into thirds. Line cookie sheets with aluminum foil, plain brown paper, parchment paper or "letter paper" (typing or airmail paper). Grind the blanched almonds fine, using a food processor, blender or nut grinder. If using a blender, the nuts may gum up and stick together; in that case strain them. Combine almonds and sugar, mixing well. Beat the egg whites briefly, add cream of tartar and salt, and continue to beat the whites until stiff but not dry. Add the almond extract toward the end of the beating process. Fold the whites into the almond sugar mixture.

Macaroons can be formed by placing slightly rounded table-spoons of the almond mixture about ½ inch apart on the prepared sheets (they don't spread). However, they are much more elegant if formed with a pastry bag fitted with a plain or star-shaped tube. Make rounds about 1 ½ inches in diameter and place them about ½ inch apart. Decorate them with ½ glacéed cherry, or a whole almond, or a few slivered almonds. Some recipes suggest sprinkling them with confectioners' sugar and letting them stand for 1 hour before baking. They are really sweet enough without the additional sugar and I haven't found that letting them stand makes an appreciable difference in texture.

Bake the macaroons for about 30 minutes, or until lightly colored. After about 20 minutes, reverse the sheets from the upper to the lower rack and turn them from front to back. Slide the foil liners off the cookie sheets and let the macaroons stand on the sheets for about 5 minutes or so. Carefully peel the foil away from the backs of the macaroons and transfer them to a rack to cool. If using brown paper, slide it off the cookie sheets and let the macaroons cool for about 5 minutes or so. Place the brown paper on top of wet paper towels to dampen it slightly. After a minute or so, carefully lift the macaroons off the paper. Cool on a rack. If the macaroons should stick to the parchment paper, treat as with brown paper.

YIELD: 36 to 44 macaroons

VARIATIONS: Try substituting filberts or hazelnuts, or even walnuts, for the almonds.

CHOCOLATE MACAROONS: Add 6 Tablespoons unsweetened sifted cocoa powder to the egg whites toward the end of the beating. Substitute vanilla extract for the almond.

ORANGE MACAROONS: Add 2 teaspoons finely grated orange rind. Reduce almond extract to 3 or 4 drops. Add ¼ teaspoon orange extract.

SARDINIAN MACAROONS: Substitute 2 cups confectioners' sugar for the ¾ cup granulated. Substitute slivered almonds for ground almonds. Reduce almond extract to ¼ teaspoon.

MACAROON SLICES: Reduce the sugar to ½ cup. Form the dough into a long roll about 1½ inches in diameter, and make a deep indentation lengthwise on the top of the roll; use the handle of a wooden spoon or a wet finger.

Bake the roll for 20 to 25 minutes, or until lightly colored. While the roll is baking, heat 1½ cups of jam (apricot, raspberry, peach, etc.) until boiling hot and very thick. When roll is done, fill the indentation with the jam and let cool slightly. Loosen the roll on the baking sheet and let it cool completely. Cut it into diagonal ½-inch slices.

YIELD: 36 slices

NOTE: Almond paste can be purchased in cans or foil packages (see Almond Paste, p. 13). If using almond paste, combine 8 ounces paste with unbeaten egg whites; then beat the mixture hard. Reduce the sugar to ½ cup or less and use only a few drops of almond extract.

Coconut Macaroons

Nice and chewy, these usually disappear very fast.

3 or 4 egg whites (½ cup)
¼ teaspoon cream of tartar
Pinch of salt
¾ to 1 cup granulated sugar

½ teaspoon almond extract
½ teaspoon vanilla extract
7 ounce flaked or shredded coconut
(2 cups packed)

Preheat oven to 325°F., and adjust the racks to divide the oven into thirds. Butter and flour cookie sheets and knock off the excess flour, or line sheets with foil.

Beat egg whites lightly, add the cream of tartar and salt, and continue to beat until soft peaks form. Gradually add the sugar, a few tablespoons at a time. Add both extracts. Beat until the whites are stiff but not dry. Fold in the coconut. Using a teaspoon and a rubber spatula, or a second teaspoon, place lightly rounded teaspoons of the meringue about 2 inches apart on the prepared cookie sheets.

Bake for 18 to 20 minutes, or until lightly colored. After about 10 minutes, reverse the sheets from the upper to the lower rack, and turn them from front to back. Let macaroons cool on the cookie sheets, or on the foil liner only, for about 5 minutes, or until macaroons can be moved to a rack to cool.

YIELD: 48 macaroons
VARIATION:

CHOCOLATE COCONUT: Increase sugar to 1¼ cups. Sift 6 Tablespoons unsweetened cocoa powder into the egg whites near the end of the beating.

V's Favorite Pine-Nut Cookies (Pignolini)

My very good friend V. is always very happy when I make these, and so am I.
They are real contenders for the number one spot on my favorite cookie list.

½ pound blanched almonds
2 cups granulated sugar
4 egg whites
Pinch of salt

1 teaspoon vanilla extract
½ pound pignoli (pine nuts)
Powdered sugar (optional)

Preheat oven to 400°F., and place a rack at the upper middle level.
Butter and flour 2 cookie sheets, knocking off excess flour, or line
them with foil. You will only bake one sheet at a time so you could
instead prepare pieces of foil the size of the cookie sheets and use
only one sheet. Grind the almonds very fine in a food processor
and combine with 1 cup of the sugar. If you are using a blender, do
no more than ½ cup of almonds at a time. If they become lumpy,
strain them before adding sugar. Beat the egg whites, adding the
salt, until they form soft peaks. Continue to beat, while gradually
adding remaining sugar and the vanilla, until the meringue holds
firm peaks and is stiff but not dry. Fold the meringue into the
almond sugar paste.

Spread the pignoli out on a large flat platter, baking pan or
jelly-roll pan. Using a heaping teaspoon of dough for each cookie,
form cookies with a spoon and a rubber spatula, or 2 spoons. Drop
the cookies, 2 or 3 at a time, on top of the pine nuts. With your
fingers, gently turn the cookies to coat them with nuts, pressing
gently to embed the nuts in the dough. Place the cookies 2 inches
apart on the prepared cookie sheets. Bake the macaroons for about
15 minutes, until pine nuts appear golden brown and cookies are
very lightly colored. After about 10 minutes, turn the cookie sheet
from back to front. Transfer the cookies to a rack to cool. Dust
with the powdered sugar, if you use it, before macaroons are
completely cool. Dust again when serving.

YIELD: 48 macaroons

Peanut Macaroons

This recipe comes from The Hermon Cookbook, *published in 1916 by the ladies of Hermon, New York, which is a small town in St. Lawrence County with a population of less than 200. Old cookbooks are fascinating reading. Quantities are often given in terms of cost and refer to ingredients no longer in use such as "five cents worth of baker's ammonia."*

2 egg whites, at room temperature	¼ teaspoon baking powder
Pinch of cream of tartar	¾ cup confectioners' sugar
2 Tablespoons all-purpose flour	1 cup chopped unsalted peanuts

Preheat oven to 325°F., and adjust the racks to divide the oven into thirds. Butter and flour 2 cookie sheets and set them aside. Beat the egg whites until they start to foam. Add the cream of tartar and beat until stiff but not dry. Combine the flour, baking powder and confectioners' sugar and gradually add this to the egg whites while still beating them. Fold in the peanuts and drop by rounded teaspoons onto the prepared cookie sheets.

Bake for 20 to 25 minutes, until the cookies are barely colored. Loosen the cookies with a spatula but let them stand on the sheets until cool.

YIELD: 40 cookies

Bars and Squares

Almond Squares

A thin crisp cracker with the texture of the ground almonds, blended with a light cinnamon flavor.

1 cup sifted all-purpose flour
¼ pound (1 stick) unsalted butter
½ cup granulated sugar
1 egg, separated

¼ teaspoon vanilla extract
½ cup ground blanched almonds
¼ cup confectioners' sugar
¼ teaspoon ground cinnamon

Preheat oven to 400° F., and place a rack at the middle level. Butter a standard cookie sheet, or line it with foil. Sift the flour before measuring and resift it; set it aside. Cream the butter with the granulated sugar until very light and fluffy. Add the egg yolk and vanilla extract and beat well. Gradually add the flour and finally the almonds. Spread the dough out as evenly as possible on the cookie sheet, using a long metal spatula or the flat side of a long knife. Constantly wetting the spatula with cold water, smooth the surface of the dough. Beat the egg white until stiff but not dry, and gradually add the mixed confectioners' sugar and cinnamon. Spread on the dough in a thin, even layer.

Bake for 12 to 15 minutes, until cookies are a very light brown, making sure the edges don't burn. Halfway through the baking time, reverse the cookie sheets. Gently loosen the baked dough from the cookie sheet and slide it onto a cutting board. While the baked dough is still warm, cut it into squares or diamond shapes and transfer these to a rack to cool.

YIELD: 48 squares, 2-inch size

Applesauce Walnut Bars

These would keep well if they weren't eaten up first.

2 cups sifted all-purpose flour
1 teaspoon baking soda
½ teaspoon ground cinnamon
¼ teaspoon ground cloves
¼ teaspoon ground nutmeg
¼ pound (1 stick) unsalted butter

¾ cup sugar
1 egg, lightly beaten
½ teaspoon vanilla extract
1 cup applesauce
2/3 cup chopped walnuts
½ cup chopped raisins

Preheat oven to 350°F. Butter and flour a square pan, 8 x 8 x 2 inches. Sift the flour before measuring and resift it with the baking soda and spices into a large bowl. Melt the butter and combine it with the sugar and beaten eggs. Add vanilla and applesauce. Add this mixture to the flour and mix it in thoroughly. Fold in the walnuts and raisins and turn the mixture into the prepared cake pan.

Bake on the middle level of the preheated oven for about 1 hour, or until a cake tester inserted into the center of the cake comes out clean. Let it cool in the pan for 10 to 15 minutes. Remove the cake from the pan and let it cool on a rack. Cut into squares or rectangles.

YIELD: 16 squares, 2-inch size, or 32 bars, 1 x 2 inches

Apricot Bars

These are moist, with a full apricot flavor.

6 ounces dried apricots (about ¾ cup)
1/3 cup granulated sugar
1 cup water
1½ cups sifted all-purpose flour
¼ teaspoon salt

6 ounces (1½ sticks) unsalted butter
½ cup firmly packed dark or light brown sugar
1 teaspoon vanilla extract
Optional: confectioners' sugar for top

Combine the apricots, granulated sugar and water in a small heavy saucepan over low heat. Cook for about 20 minutes, stirring occasionally, until the apricots are tender and most of the liquid has been absorbed. Purée the fruit in a food processor or blender, or force the fruit through a strainer, and set it aside.

Preheat oven to 350°F. Butter and flour a square pan 9 x 9 x 2 inches, and shake out the excess flour. Sift the flour before measuring it and resift it with the salt. Cream the butter with the brown sugar until mixture is light. Beat in the vanilla and gradually add the sifted flour and salt, mixing just until incorporated. Turn the batter into the prepared pan, leveling it with a spatula. Spread the apricot purée on top in an even layer.

Bake in the middle level of the preheated oven for 25 to 30 minutes, or until a cake tester inserted in the center comes out clean. Cool in the pan placed on a rack before cutting into bars 1 x 2¼ inches. Sprinkle with confectioners' sugar or leave plain if you prefer.

YIELD: 36 bars
VARIATION: Sprinkle the tops with slivered almonds or shredded coconut.

Brownies

The classic that seems to be everyone's favorite.

½ cup sifted all-purpose flour
¼ teaspoon salt
3 ounces (¾ stick) unsalted butter
1 cup granulated sugar
2 eggs

2 ounces (2 squares) unsweetened
   chocolate, melted and cooled
   slightly
½ teaspoon vanilla extract
1 cup walnut or pecan halves or
   large pieces

Preheat oven to 325°F., and place a rack at the middle level. Butter a square pan, 8 x 8 x 2 inches, line it with wax paper, butter and flour the paper, and shake off excess flour. Sift the flour before measuring and resift it with the salt. Cream the butter and beat in the sugar. Add the eggs one at a time, beating after each addition. Stir in the chocolate and beat in the vanilla. Add the sifted dry ingredients and beat until just mixed. Fold in the nuts and turn mixture into the prepared pan.

   Bake for 25 to 30 minutes. Brownies should be moist; they are done when a cake tester inserted in the center comes out barely clean. Allow them to cool in the pan for about 30 minutes. Place a rack or cookie sheet over the pan and invert it. Remove the pan and the wax paper, cover with another rack or cookie sheet, and invert again. Slide onto a cutting board. With a thin sharp knife cut into 2-inch squares or bars 1 x 2 inches.

YIELD: 16 squares, 2-inch size, or 32 bars, 1 x 2 inches
NOTE: Some recipes call for ½ teaspoon baking powder. This results in less dense brownies, but you might prefer them.

Katharine Hepburn's Brownies

That fine actress is justifiably proud of her brownies. They are wonderful frozen and can be eaten right from the freezer. Also delicious eaten while they are still warm.

¼ pound (1 stick) unsalted butter
2 ounces (2 squares) unsweetened
   chocolate
1 cup granulated sugar
2 eggs

½ teaspoon vanilla extract
1 cup roughly chopped walnuts
¼ cup (or less) *un*sifted all-
   purpose flour

Preheat oven to 325°F. Butter a square pan 8 x 8 x 2 inches, line it with wax paper, and butter the paper. In a heavy saucepan melt the butter with the chocolate. Remove from the heat and let cool briefly. Add the sugar, stirring it in. Add the eggs one at a time, beating well after each addition. Beat in the vanilla, walnuts and flour. Pour into the prepared pan. Miss Hepburn cautions: "Work fast after adding the eggs. The mixture should be stiff enough to want to stand."

Bake on the middle level of the preheated oven for 40 to 45 minutes. Let cool in the pan for about 30 minutes. Place a rack or cookie sheet over the pan and invert it. Remove the pan and the wax paper, cover with another rack or cookie sheet and invert again. Transfer to a cutting board. With a thin sharp knife, cut into 2-inch squares or 1 x 2 inch bars.

YIELD: 16 squares, 2-inch size, or 32 bars, 1 x 2 inches

Butterscotch Brownies

It may come as a great shock to the chocoholics of the world but there are some people who prefer butterscotch brownies to chocolate ones. For those who are not of this persuasion, a sampling of these may change their minds.

3 ounces (¾ stick) unsalted butter
¾ cup firmly packed dark brown
    sugar
1 egg, beaten
1 teaspoon vanilla extract
¾ cup sifted all-purpose flour

1 teaspoon baking powder
¼ teaspoon salt
¾ cup coarsely chopped nuts

Preheat oven to 350°F., and place a rack at the middle level. Butter a baking pan 8 x 8 x 2 inches, line it with wax paper, and butter the paper. Cream the butter until it is soft. Add the sugar, beating until the mixture is fluffy. Add the egg and the vanilla and beat well. Resift the flour with the baking powder and salt and add it to the batter. Fold in the nuts and scrape the batter into the prepared baking pan.

Bake for about 30 minutes, or until a toothpick inserted in the center comes out clean. The brownies should be moist in the middle. Allow them to cool completely in the pan, about 30 minutes. Place a rack or cookie sheet over the pan and invert it. Remove the pan and the wax paper. Cover with a rack and invert again. Transfer to a cutting board. With a thin sharp knife, cut into long strips and then crosswise into squares.

YIELD: 16 squares, 2-inch size, or 32 bars, 1 x 2 inches

Cocoa Brownies

These are very quick to make, particularly if you use a food processor, as they call for cocoa rather than melted chocolate.

½ cup sifted all-purpose flour
6 Tablespoons unsweetened cocoa
  powder
¼ teaspoon salt
¼ pound (1 stick) unsalted butter

¾ cup granulated sugar
2 eggs, lightly beaten
1 teaspoon vanilla extract
½ cup coarsely chopped walnuts or
  pecans

Preheat oven to 350°F., and place a rack at the middle level. Butter a pan 8 x 8 x 2 inches, line it with wax paper, and butter the paper. Sift the flour before measuring and resift it with the cocoa and salt. Cream the butter and sugar until light and fluffy. Beat in the eggs and vanilla and blend well. Add the flour gradually until it is thoroughly mixed. (In the food processor, add the flour all at once and process with 4 or 5 on/off turns.) Fold in the nuts. Turn the mixture into the prepared pan, leveling it with a spatula.

Bake for 25 to 30 minutes, or until a cake tester comes out clean. Allow the cake to cool in the pan for about 30 minutes. Place a rack or cookie sheet over the pan and invert it. Remove the pan and wax paper. Cover with another rack and invert again. Transfer to a cutting board. With a thin sharp knife, cut into long strips and then crosswise into squares or bars.

YIELD: 16 squares, 2-inch size, or 32 bars, 1 x 2 inches

Butterfudge Fingers

This recipe is a contribution from our old friend "Anonymous." The card, neatly typed, was in my recipe files. The recipe makes a delicious rich brownie-type bar, but I don't know whom to thank for it!

2 ounces (2 squares) unsweetened chocolate	¾ cup sifted all-purpose flour
3¼ ounces (2/3 stick) butter	½ teaspoon baking powder
1 cup granulated sugar	½ teaspoon salt
2 eggs	½ cup broken nut meats

Topping

2 ounces (½ stick) unsalted butter	2 Tablespoons cream
2 cups sifted confectioners' sugar	1 teaspoon vanilla extract

Icing

1 ounce (1 square) unsweetened chocolate	1 Tablespoon butter

Preheat oven to 350°F., and place a rack at the middle level. Butter a pan 9 x 9 x 2 inches or 11¼ x 7½ inches. Line the bottom of the pan with wax paper and butter the paper. In a saucepan over low heat, or in the top part of a double boiler over hot water, melt the chocolate with the butter. Remove from heat and beat in the sugar and the eggs. Sift the flour before measuring and resift it with the baking powder and salt. Combine dry ingredients with the chocolate mixture. Fold in the nuts and spread the mixture in the prepared pan.

Bake for 25 to 30 minutes, until the top has a slightly dull look. Cool slightly, about 15 minutes. Place a rack or cookie sheet over the pan and invert it. Remove the pan and the wax paper, cover with another rack, and invert the cake again to cool completely.

While the cake is cooling, prepare the topping: Melt the butter over medium heat until it is lightly browned; watch carefully so that it does not burn. Remove butter from the heat and beat it into the confectioners' sugar. Blend in the cream and vanilla. Spread the mixture on the brownies.

Prepare the icing: Melt the chocolate with the butter over low heat or over hot water, and allow it to cool. Spread it in a very thin coating over the topping.

Since this is really rich, cut it into small pieces: 1-inch squares or fingers 1 x 1½ inches.

YIELD: 81 squares, 1-inch size, or 54 fingers, 1 x 1½ inches

Chocolate Chip Nut Bars

These are as good as they sound and quick and easy to make.

2 ½ cups sifted all-purpose flour
½ teaspoon salt
¼ pound (1 stick) unsalted butter
1 ½ cups firmly packed dark brown
   sugar
3 eggs

1 teaspoon vanilla extract
6 ounces semisweet chocolate bits
1 cup coarsely chopped pecans or
   walnuts
½ cup raisins (optional)
Confectioners' sugar (optional)

Preheat oven to 350°F., and place a rack at the middle level. Butter a jelly-roll pan 10 x 15 inches. Sift the flour before measuring and mix in the salt. Cream the butter until light. Beat in the sugar until the mixture is creamy. Add the eggs one at a time, beating well after each addition. Stir in the vanilla and gradually add the flour, blending it in. Fold in the chocolate bits and nuts, and raisins if you use them. Turn batter into the prepared pan.

Bake for 30 to 35 minutes, until the top springs back when gently touched. Cool in the pan on a rack before cutting with a thin sharp knife into bars or squares. Dust with confectioners' sugar, if you like, before serving.

YIELD: 40 bars, 1½ x 2 ½ inches

Chocolate Nut Bars

This is a richly satisfying super brownie that is baked on a cookie sheet.

1 cup sifted all-purpose flour
1 teaspoon baking powder
⅛ teaspoon salt
3 tablespoons unsalted butter
3 ounces (3 squares) unsweetened
  chocolate

1 egg, beaten
1 cup granulated sugar
½ cup chopped pecans, walnuts
  or other nuts
1 teaspoon vanilla extract

Preheat oven to 375°F, and place a rack at the middle level. Butter a baking sheet or flat pan 17 x 14 inches. If you don't have one, invert a rectangular roasting pan or lasagna pan and butter the bottom of it. Sift the flour before measuring and resift it with the baking powder and salt. Melt the butter and chocolate over very low heat, and set it aside to cool slightly. Beat the egg and gradually add the sugar, beating until thick and smooth. Stir in the melted butter and chocolate and add the sifted flour. Fold in the nuts and stir in the vanilla. Spread the batter in a very thin even layer on the prepared baking sheet.

Bake for 18 to 20 minutes, or until a slight crust forms.

Cool in the pan on a rack before cutting into squares.

YIELD: 56 squares, 2-inch size

Coconut Almond Bars

The coconut topping adds an extra touch to the almond bars, but they are delicious without any topping.

½ cup sifted all-purpose flour
¼ teaspoon salt
⅛ teaspoon baking powder
1 egg

¾ cup lightly packed brown sugar, dark or light, sifted
½ teaspoon vanilla extract
1 cup ground blanched almonds

Topping (optional)

¾ cup shredded coconut (preferably unsweetened)
1/3 cup brown sugar (less if using sweetened coconut)

3 Tablespoons melted unsalted butter
2 Tablespoons cream
Few drops of vanilla extract

Preheat oven to 325°F., and place a rack at the middle level. Butter a cake pan 8 x 8 x 2 inches. Sift the flour before measuring and resift it with the salt and baking powder. Beat the egg until it is very foamy and light. Gradually add the brown sugar and vanilla and combine well. Gradually stir in the flour mixture and then the almonds. Scrape the mixture into the prepared pan and spread it level with a spatula.

Bake for 25 to 30 minutes. The top will be crusty and firm. While the cake is warm, cut it into 2-inch squares and allow them to cool in the pan.

If you are using the topping, remove the cake from the oven and increase oven heat to 375°F. Let the cake cool for about 5 minutes. Meanwhile prepare the topping by combining all ingredients. Spread evenly on the slightly cooled cake and place the cake under the broiler for 2 or 3 minutes to brown lightly. Watch that it does not burn. Cut into squares while it is still warm.

YIELD: 16 squares, 2-inch size

Coconut Pecan Bars

This two-stage recipe makes a chewy crunchy morsel.

1 cup sifted all-purpose flour
¼ pound (1 stick) unsalted butter
½ cup lightly packed dark brown
  sugar
2 eggs, well beaten
¾ cup light brown or granulated
  sugar

½ cup shredded coconut
2 Tablespoons all-purpose flour
1 cup coarsely chopped pecans
1 teaspoon vanilla extract
Pinch of salt

Preheat oven to 350°F., and place a rack at the middle level. Butter a square cake pan 8 x 8 x 2 inches. Sift the flour before measuring. Cream the butter with the dark brown sugar, add the flour, and mix thoroughly. Scrape this batter into the prepared pan, spreading it evenly into the corners. Bake for 20 minutes.

While the first layer is baking, prepare the topping. Beat the eggs until they are foamy; add the light brown sugar and beat until thick. Toss the coconut with the flour and add it and the pecans to the egg and sugar mixture. Beat in the vanilla and the pinch of salt. Mix well. Spread this mixture evenly over the baked layer and return the pan to the oven for an additional 20 minutes, or until the top is nicely browned. Cool the cake in the pan and cut into squares or bars.

YIELD: 16 squares, 2-inch size, or 32 bars, 1 x 2 inches

Date Nut Bars I

Moist and very satisfying, nice with a cup of coffee or tea. Extra rich with the topping, but still good without it.

1 cup chopped dates (8 ounces)
1 cup boiling water
1 teaspoon baking soda
1½ cups sifted all-purpose flour
1 teaspoon baking powder
½ teaspoon salt

2½ ounces (2/3 stick) unsalted butter
1 cup granulated sugar
1 egg
1 teaspoon vanilla extract
2 ounces chopped nuts (½ cup)

Topping

¼ cup firmly packed light or dark brown sugar
5 Tablespoons heavy cream

2 ounces (½ stick) unsalted butter
¾ cup chopped nuts or coconut, or half of each

Preheat oven to 350°F., and place a rack at the middle level. Butter and flour a pan 8 x 8 x 2 inches. If the dates are whole, cut them up with a heavy knife or scissors, and place them in a small bowl. Pour the boiling water over them and add the baking soda. Set aside to cool. Sift the flour before measuring and resift it with the baking powder and salt. Cream the butter until soft. Beat in the sugar until light and fluffy. Beat in the egg. Gradually add the sifted dry ingredients, stirring until blended in. Stir in the vanilla. Add the cooled dates and their liquid. Turn the batter into the prepared pan.

Bake for about 35 to 40 minutes, until the top springs back when gently pressed with a fingertip, and a cake tester inserted in the center comes out clean.

Prepare the topping shortly before the cake is finished baking. In a small saucepan over moderate heat, combine the brown sugar, cream, butter and nuts and/or coconut. Bring to a boil and boil for 3 minutes. When the cake is done, remove it from the oven and increase the heat to broil, or heat your separate broiler. Spread the topping over the hot cake and place it under the broiler for about 2 minutes. Watch that it doesn't burn. Cool in the pan on a rack before cutting into bars.

YIELD: 32 bars, 1 x 2 inches

Date Nut Bars II

These are made with honey, which makes them long lasting. Theoretically, they will stay fresh for 2 or 3 weeks but I haven't been able to keep them that long.

2 cups ground pitted dates
1 cup coarsely chopped nuts
   (walnuts or pecans)
1½ cups sifted all-purpose flour
1 teaspoon baking powder

½ teaspoon salt
3 eggs
1 cup honey
Confectioners' sugar (optional)

Preheat oven to 350°F., and place a rack at the middle level. Butter and flour one pan 9 x 13 inches or two pans 6 x 10 inches. Sift the flour before measuring and resift it with the baking powder and salt. Beat the eggs until foamy. Gradually stir in the honey. Add the sifted dry ingredients, stirring them in well. Stir in the dates and nuts. Turn the batter into the prepared pan.

Bake for about 30 minutes until cake is lightly crusted and top springs back when gently pressed with a fingertip. A cake tester inserted in the center should come out clean. Cool in the pan on a rack. Cut into bars. Sprinkle with confectioners' sugar if desired.

YIELD: 45 bars, 1 x 2½ inches

Duxbury Cheesecake Squares

A contribution from my friend Mariza, who lives in that old historic town near Plymouth Rock. It is a mystery to me how she remains so slim and can still eat this calorie contributor.

1 cup sifted all-purpose flour
¼ teaspoon salt
1/3 cup melted unsalted butter

1/3 cup firmly packed dark or light brown sugar
4 ounces finely chopped nuts (1 cup)

Filling

8 ounces cream cheese, softened
¼ cup granulated sugar
1 Tablespoon lemon juice

1½ teaspoons vanilla extract
1 egg
3 Tablespoons light cream or milk

Preheat oven to 350°F., and place a rack at the middle level. Butter a square pan 8 x 8 x 2 inches. Sift the flour before measuring and stir in the salt. Combine the melted butter with the brown sugar and beat until smooth and creamy. Add the flour, mixing it in well, and finally the ground nuts. Press half of this mixture into the prepared pan. Reserve the rest for the top. Bake for about 15 minutes or until color is a light golden.

While the pastry is baking prepare the filling. Beat the softened cream cheese with the sugar. Beat in the lemon juice and vanilla. Beat the egg and cream or milk together thoroughly and mix it into the cheese and sugar.

When pastry is baked, remove pan from the oven, but do not turn off oven. Let the pastry cool briefly before spreading the top with the cream-cheese mixture. Spread on the reserved pastry and return the pan to the oven. Bake for an additional 25 minutes, or until set. Cool in the pan on a rack before cutting into squares or bars.

YIELD: 16 squares, 2-inch size, or 32 bars, 1 x 2 inches

Foxy Fruit Bars

I christened them "foxy" because their very nice flavor comes from some high-protein ingedients. These are not too sweet. The tang from the apricots goes well with the chocolate.

1¾ cups sifted all-purpose flour
½ cup sifted whole-wheat pastry
   flour
1/3 cup sifted or unsifted soy
   flour
1 teaspoon baking powder
1 teaspoon baking soda
½ teaspoon salt
1 teaspoon ground cinnamon
½ teaspoon ground cloves
½ teaspoon ground nutmeg
¼ teaspoon ground allspice
6 ounces (1½ sticks) unsalted
   butter

1 cup firmly packed dark brown
   sugar
½ cup granulated sugar
2 eggs
1½ teaspoons vanilla extract
½ cup unsweetened cocoa powder
¼ cup powdered nonfat dry milk
1 cup plain yogurt
1 cup old-fashioned rolled oats
1 cup slivered almonds
1 cup dried apricots, cut up
½ cup raisins or currants
Powdered sugar (for topping)

Preheat oven to 350°F., and place a rack at the middle level. Butter and flour a jelly-roll pan, approximately 10 x 15 inches. Shake out the excess flour. Sift the all-purpose and whole-wheat flours before measuring, then resift with the soy flour, baking powder, baking soda, salt and spices. In a large mixing bowl, cream the butter with both sugars until light and fluffy. Add the eggs one at a time, beating after each addition. Add the vanilla, then beat in the cocoa and the dry milk. Alternately add the yogurt and the sifted dry ingredients, just until mixed. Stir in the oats, almonds, apricots and raisins. The mixture will be quite stiff. Spread the dough evenly in the prepared pan.

Bake in the middle level of the preheated oven for 30 to 35 minutes, or until a cake tester inserted in the center comes out clean. The top will be slightly crusted. Cool the cake in the pan, on a rack, before cutting into squares or bars. Sprinkle bars with powdered sugar before serving.

YIELD: 40 squares, 2-inch size, each containing about 5 grams of protein (about 10 percent of the adult R. D. A.)
VARIATION: Instead of powdered sugar, spread with coconut topping (see Coconut Almond Bars, p. 152).

Gerta's Old-Fashioned Raisin Squares

Gerta Kessler is a delightful woman who is an excellent and loving cook and a good friend of mine. Presently living in Florida, she is a Pennsylvanian who lived for many years in Pottstown, enjoying all the good food that region grows. For another delectable sweet of hers, see the Small Yeast Cookies (p. 114).

1 cup seedless raisins
1 cup water
¼ pound (1 stick) unsalted butter
   (see Note)
1 cup granulated sugar
1 egg, lightly beaten
1¾ cups sifted all-purpose flour

¼ teaspoon salt
¼ teaspoon baking powder
¼ teaspoon ground allspice
¼ teaspoon ground cinnamon
¼ teaspoon ground nutmeg
½ cup chopped nuts
Confectioners' sugar (optional)

Preheat oven to 350°F., and place a rack at the middle level. Butter and flour a pan 13 x 9 x 2 inches; shake out the excess flour. In a saucepan over moderate heat, combine raisins and water and bring just to the boil. Remove from heat, stir in the butter, and cool the mixture to lukewarm. Stir the sugar and beaten egg into the raisin mixture. Sift the flour before measuring and resift it with the salt, baking powder and spices. Beat it into the batter and fold in the nuts. Turn the batter into the prepared pan.

Bake the cake in the preheated oven for about 30 minutes, or until a cake tester inserted in the center comes out clean. Let cool in the pan before cutting into squares. After cake is cool, dust with confectioners' sugar if you use it.

YIELD: 48 squares, 1½-inch size
NOTE: The butter is my version. Gerta uses liquid shortening.

Ginger Almond Bars

These are really special, with a rich, moist flavor.

1¾ cups sifted all-purpose flour
⅛ teaspoon salt
½ pound (2 sticks) unsalted butter
1 cup granulated sugar
1 egg
1 Tablespoon grated orange rind

½ cup preserved gingerroot, finely chopped and drained of syrup
2 Tablespoons Amaretto liqueur or rum or brandy *or* 2 Tablespoons orange juice and ¼ teaspoon almond extract
½ cup very finely chopped almonds

Preheat oven to 350°F., and place a rack at the middle level. Butter a pan 9 x 9 x 2 inches. Sift the flour before measuring and stir in the salt. Cream the butter with the sugar until light and fluffy. Beat in the egg and orange rind. Gradually add the sifted flour until just incorporated. Stir in the liqueur, or juice and almond extract, and fold in the gingerroot and nuts. Turn the mixture into the prepared pan, leveling the top with a spatula.

Bake for 25 to 30 minutes, or until lightly browned. A cake tester inserted in the center should come out clean. Cool in the pan on a rack before cutting into bars or squares.

YIELD: 18 bars, 1½ x 3 inches, or 36 squares, 1½-inch size

Lemon Bars

These have a lovely tang to them. Please use fresh lemon juice only because the flavor is just not the same when any subsitute is used.

¼ pound (1 stick) unsalted butter   1 cup sifted all-purpose flour
¼ cup confectioners' sugar

Topping

2 Tablespoons fresh lemon juice   2 eggs, beaten
Grated rind of 1 lemon   2 teaspoons all-purpose flour
¾ cup granulated sugar   ½ teaspoon baking powder

Preheat oven to 350°F., and place a rack at the middle level. Butter a pan 9 x 13 inches. Cream the butter with the sugar and beat in the sifted flour. Scrape batter into the buttered pan, leveling dough with a flexible spatula. Bake for 15 minutes and remove the pan to cool slightly. Do not turn off the oven.

While the first layer is cooling, mix the lemon juice, rind and sugar, then beat in the eggs. Combine flour and baking powder and sift the mixture over the sugar and eggs, mixing it very well. Spread topping over the cooled baked layer and return the pan to the oven. Bake for an additional 20 to 25 minutes. Allow the pastry to cool before cutting into bars or squares.

YIELD: 48 squares, 1½-inch size

Lois's Heavenly Bars

Lois is the grandmother of an attractive young baby named Henry, and he is still too young to try these, but he will undoubtedly love them when he grows a bit more.

2 cups sifted all-purpose flour
2 teaspoons baking soda
2 teaspoons ground cinnamon
½ teaspoon salt
5 ounces (1¼ sticks) unsalted butter

1 2/3 cups granulated sugar
3 eggs
3 jars (4 oz. each) strained baby food, 1 apricot, 1 applesauce, 1 carrot

Topping (optional)

3 ounces cream cheese
3 Tablespoons unsalted butter

1 1/3 cups confectioners' sugar

Preheat oven to 350° F., and place a rack at the middle level. Butter a jelly-roll pan 10 x 15 inches. Sift the flour before measuring and resift t with the baking soda, cinnamon and salt. Cream the butter and sugar until light and fluffy. Add the eggs one at a time, beating after each addition. Beat in the strained baby foods, mixing well. Gradually add the sifted dry ingredients and beat just until incorporated. Spread the mixture evenly over the greased pan.

Bake for 28 to 35 minutes, or until the top springs back when gently pressed with a finger. Cool in the pan on a rack before spreading with the topping. To make the topping, cream the cream cheese and butter until they are completely blended and then work in the confectioners' sugar gradually. Spread in a thin layer with a spatula. Cut the cake into squares or bars.

YIELD: 50 bars, 2 x 1½ inches

Newton Twins

Once you've made these, you will never again be happy with store-bought fig newtons. These are luscious, with a generous filling. The apricot version is just as good, I think. Make both and decide! A food processor is a big help in this recipe.

3 cups sifted all-purpose flour
1 teaspoon baking powder
½ teaspoon baking soda
½ teaspoon ground cinnamon
½ teaspoon salt
5 ounces (1¼ sticks) unsalted butter

½ cup firmly packed dark brown sugar
½ cup granulated sugar
2 egg whites, very lightly beaten
Filling (recipes follow)

Sift the flour before measuring and resift it with the baking powder, baking soda, cinnamon and salt. Cream the butter until soft and light. Gradually add both sugars, and beat until light and fluffy. Beat in the egg whites. Gradually add in the sifted dry ingredients, scraping the bowl with a spatula and beating until well mixed. Turn the dough out on wax paper, and divide it into halves. Wrap each half in wax paper, flatten the dough balls slightly, and place them in the refrigerator for several hours or overnight. You can also place the dough in the freezer for 1 or 2 hours until it is firm enough to roll out.

Preheat oven to 375°F., and place a rack at the upper middle level. Line a cookie sheet with foil. If you have a very large cookie sheet (14 x 17 inches) line the sheet with 2 pieces of foil. If your cookie sheet is the standard 12 x 16 you will have to bake the Newtons half at a time.

Remove one package of dough from the refrigerator. If the dough has hardened too much, beat it with a rolling pin to soften it slightly. Use a floured pastry cloth and floured rolling pin, or place dough between 2 sheets of wax paper. Roll the dough out ¼ inch thick. Shape it into a rectangle 15 inches long and 6 inches wide. Measure it for accuracy and trim it evenly, patching where necessary with the trimmed dough. Work fast as the dough softens rapidly. If it becomes too soft, refrigerate it or pop it into the freezer for a few minutes until it is again firm enough to work with.

Remove one of the fillings from the refrigerator. Using a spoon and a rubber spatula, or 2 spoons, spread the filling lengthwise down the center of the dough about 1 inch thick and 2 inches wide, stopping ½ inch from each of the narrow ends. Smooth the filling with a spatula (a food processor plastic spatula is just 2 inches wide and works well here), but don't flatten it. The two long sides of the pastry are now to be folded over the filling and they should overlap each other by ¼ to ½ inch. Use the pastry cloth to lift the dough. Press gently to seal the overlap. If you are using wax paper, slide the wax paper and dough onto a tea towel which will help support the wax paper as you overlap the long edges over the filling. Again using the pastry cloth, or tea towel and wax paper, turn the filled dough over so it has the seam side down. Slide it onto the foil-lined cookie sheet lengthwise in the center of the sheet. If the cookie sheet is too short, place the dough diagonally on the sheet. Smooth out the log with your hands to even it and press down lightly on the 2 ends to seal them.

Bake for 12 to 15 minutes, or until the log is an even golden brown. After 8 or 9 minutes, reverse the cookie sheet from front to back. When done, slide the foil off the cookie sheet and let the log remain on the foil for about 10 minutes, or until it is firm enough to be removed. With your hands carefully transfer it to a rack to cool.

Prepare the second half of the dough in the same way and place on a sheet of foil. Bake when the first log is finished. The logs will slice more easily if they are refrigerated briefly when cool. Use a thin sharp knife or a finely serrated one and cut the log crosswise into 1-inch slices, wiping the blade with a damp cloth or paper towel as necessary.

You can form the Newtons individually if you prefer. Roll the dough out ¼ inch thick and cut into pieces about 3 x 2½ inches. Place a rounded teaspoon of filling in the center and fold the side pieces over the filling, overlapping them (like folding a business letter). Flatten them slightly and place them seam side down about 1 inch apart on an ungreased or foil-lined cookie sheet. Bake at 350°F. for about 12 minutes, or until brown and just firm.

YIELD: 30 log slices, 1 x 3 inches, or about 36 individual Newtons, 1 x 2½ inches

NOTE: Bakers' supply shops and certain specialty shops carry a thick stiff fruit filling called *lekvar*. It comes in both prune and apricot (see Sources, p. 224). If you prefer, use *lekvar* instead of the filling recipes that follow.

Fig Filling

12 ounces dried figs
2 Tablespoons granulated sugar
2 Tablespoons plus 2 teaspoons
 lemon juice

2 Tablespoons plus 2 teaspoons
 orange juice
1 cup water

Cut the stems off the figs. Chop the figs very fine with a heavy chef's knife or in a food processor or meat grinder. There should be 1¼ to 1½ cups. In a heavy saucepan combine the figs with the sugar, lemon and orange juices and the water. Do not let mixture boil, but simmer it, stirring frequently, for 8 to 10 minutes, until it is thick. Turn out onto a large piece of wax paper and spread it out in a shallow layer. Let it cool at room temperature; then refrigerate it.

Apricot Filling

12 ounces dried apricots
¾ cup honey
2 Tablespoons lemon juice

2 Tablespoons plus 2 teaspoons
 orange juice
¼ cup water

Prepare the apricot filling by chopping the apricots fine or grinding them. There should be about 1½ cups. In a heavy saucepan combine the apricots with the honey, lemon and orange juices and the water. Simmer the mixture, stirring frequently, for about 10 minutes, until thick. Turn out onto a large piece of wax paper and spread it out in a shallow layer. Let it cool at room temperature; then refrigerate it.

NOTE: Both fillings can be prepared several days in advance.

Oatmeal Raisin Squares

These have a comforting old-fashioned taste. If you want them richer, spread them with the topping for Date Nut Bars I (p. 154).

1¼ cups boiling water
1 cup rolled oats (preferably old-fashioned)
1½ cups sifted all-purpose flour
1 teaspoon baking soda
½ teaspoon salt
½ teaspoon ground cinnamon
¼ teaspoon ground nutmeg
⅛ teaspoon ground cloves

¼ pound (1 stick) unsalted butter
1½ cups granulated sugar, *or* ¾ cup firmly packed dark brown sugar *and* ¾ cup granulated sugar
1 teaspoon vanilla extract
2 eggs
1 cup raisins
Confectioners' sugar (optional)

Pour the boiling water over the oats. Set them aside, covered, for 20 minutes. Preheat oven to 350°F., and place a rack at the middle level. Butter and flour a pan 8 x 8 x 2 inches and shake out the excess flour. Sift the flour before measuring and resift it with the baking soda, salt and all the spices. In a large bowl cream the butter until soft. Beat in the sugar, or sugars, until light and fluffy. Beat in the vanilla and add the eggs one at a time, beating after each addition. Stir in the oats. Gradually add the sifted dry ingredients, mixing just until incorporated. Fold in the raisins. Turn the batter into the prepared pan.

Bake for 45 to 55 minutes, until top springs back when gently pressed with a fingertip and the edges of the cake have pulled away from the pan. Dust with confectioners' sugar, if you use it, while cake is still warm. Let it cool in the pan before cutting into squares.

YIELD: 16 squares, 2-inch size, or 32 bars, 1 x 2 inches

Peanut-Butter Oatmeal Bars

Children love these and their parents seem to agree.

1 cup sifted all-purpose flour
½ teaspoon baking soda
½ teaspoon salt
¼ pound (1 stick) unsalted butter
½ cup granulated sugar
½ cup firmly packed dark brown
  sugar

1/3 cup peanut butter, preferably
  crunchy
1 egg
1 teaspoon vanilla extract
¼ cup milk
1 cup rolled oats, preferably
  old-fashioned

Preheat oven to 350°F., and place a rack at the middle level. Butter a pan 9 x 13 inches and set it aside. Sift the flour before measuring it and resift it with the baking soda and salt. Cream the butter with the sugars until light and fluffy and blend in the peanut butter. Add the eggs, beating well, and then the vanilla and milk. Beat in the sifted dry ingredients until just incorporated. Add the oats and mix well. Spread the batter in the prepared pan, leveling it.

Bake for about 20 minutes, or until a cake tester inserted in the center comes out clean. Let cool in the pan, on a rack, before cutting into rectangles or squares. If you like a topping, soften chocolate morsels over hot water and spread them on the cake while it is warm. Or bring to a boil 2 ounces (½ stick) unsalted butter with ¼ cup honey. Remove from heat, add ½ cup coarsely chopped peanuts, and stir until blended. Spread this on the warm cake and place it under the broiler for a few minutes. Watch it carefully so that it doesn't burn.

YIELD: 30 squares, 2-inch size

Pecan Raspberry Bars

How could anything with raspberries be anything but absolutely delicious?

¼ pound (1 stick) unsalted butter
1/3 cup confectioners' sugar, sifted
1 cup sifted all-purpose flour
1 cup raspberry jelly or seedless raspberry jam

2 egg whites
⅛ teaspoon cream of tartar
1/3 cup granulated sugar mixed with ¼ teaspoon ground cinnamon
1 cup ground pecans or filberts

Preheat oven to 350°F., and place a rack at the middle level. Butter a pan 9 x 13 inches. Cream the butter with the confectioners' sugar until light. Stir in the flour until it is just blended. Spread the mixture in the prepared pan, spreading it level with a spatula. Bake for about 15 minutes. Remove pan from the oven, but do not turn the oven off.

Let the baked layer cool for at least 15 minutes; then spread the raspberry jelly on the top. Beat egg whites with the cream of tartar until they form soft peaks. Gradually add the granulated sugar and cinnamon, beating at the same time, until the whites are stiff but not dry. Fold in the ground nuts. Spread this meringue over the jelly. Bake for an additional 20 to 25 minutes. Do not let the meringue get too dark. Let the cake cool in the pan on a rack before cutting into bars or squares.

YIELD: about 30 squares, 2-inch size

Prune Nut Bars

These moist and satisfying bars are a favorite with children.

12 ounces dried prunes (1½ cups)
1¾ cups sifted all-purpose flour
¼ cup *un*sifted soy flour
2 teaspoons baking powder
½ teaspoon ground nutmeg
4 eggs
¾ cup granulated sugar
¾ cup firmly packed light or dark
   brown sugar
¼ teaspoon salt
2 teaspoons grated lemon rind
1 cup chopped unsalted peanuts or
   walnuts
Powdered sugar (optional)

Cover the prunes with boiling water and soak them until they are soft. Drain them thoroughly, remove the pits, and cut them into small pieces. Preheat oven to 350°F. Butter and flour a jelly-roll pan 10 x 15 inches. Sift the flour before measuring and resift it with the soy flour, baking powder and nutmeg. Beat eggs until light and foamy. Gradually add both sugars and the salt, beating until very light. Add the lemon rind. Gradually add the sifted dry ingredients, beating them in well until thoroughly blended. Add prunes and nuts. Spread the batter in the prepared pan.

Bake for 30 to 35 minutes, until top springs back when lightly pressed and cake has pulled from sides of pan. While still warm, cut into bars or squares and sprinkle with powdered sugar if you use it.

YIELD: 40 bars, 1½ x 2½ inches, or 40 squares, 2-inch size

Seedcake Bars

Recipes for this cake are found in many old cookbooks, particularly Southern ones. The brandy in this recipe is Mrs. Beeton's idea.

2 cups sifted all-purpose flour	1 cup granulated sugar
½ teaspoon ground nutmeg or mace	3 eggs
	1 Tablespoon brandy (optional)
½ teaspoon salt	2 Tablespoons caraway seeds
½ pound (2 sticks) unsalted butter	

Preheat oven to 350°F., and place a rack at the middle level. Butter a cake tin 6 x 10 x 1 inches or 8 x 8 x 2 inches. Sift the flour before measuring and resift it with the nutmeg or mace and salt. Cream the butter until soft. Add the sugar, beating until light and fluffy. Add the eggs one at a time, beating after each addition. Stir in the brandy if you use it. Gradually add the sifted flour mixture and finally the caraway seeds. Turn batter into the prepared cake pan, spreading it level.

Bake for about 45 minutes, or until cake is lightly colored and a cake tester inserted in the center comes out clean. Let cool in the pan on a rack before slicing into bars.

YIELD: 30 bars, 1 x 2 inches

VARIATION: For a slightly lighter cake, separate the eggs. Add the yolks to the butter and sugar and then fold in stiffly beaten whites before adding the flour.

Toffee Bars
Thin and slightly chewy; this recipe yields a large batch.

2 cups sifted all-purpose flour
½ pound (2 sticks) unsalted
   butter
1 cup firmly packed dark brown
   sugar

1 teaspoon vanilla extract
6 ounces semisweet chocolate
   bits
1 cup chopped walnuts

Preheat oven to 350°F., and place a rack at the middle level. Lightly butter a jelly-roll pan 10 x 15 x 1 inches. Sift the flour before measuring. Cream the butter and sugar until light and fluffy; beat in the vanilla. Add the flour gradually, beating until just mixed. Stir in chocolate bits and walnuts. Spread the mixture, which will be stiff, in the prepared pan and level it with a wet flexible spatula.

Bake for about 25 minutes, or until cake is nicely browned and faintly crusted. Let cake cool slightly before cutting it into squares or bars with a thin sharp knife. Let them cool before removing from the pan.

YIELD: 40 squares, 2-inch size, or 80 bars, 1 x 2 inches
VARIATION: Omit chocolate chips and add 1 cup raisins.

Zucchini Walnut Bars

Some people are anti-zucchini (probably because they were subjected to overcooked and waterlogged versions); it is probably unwise to tell them that this delicious treat is made with zucchini.

1½ cups sifted all-purpose flour
1 teaspoon baking powder
½ teaspoon salt
½ teaspoon ground cinnamon
2 small or 1 large zucchini (10 ounces)
¼ pound (1 stick) unsalted butter

¾ cup sugar
2 eggs
1 teaspoon vanilla extract, *or* 1 teaspoon grated lemon rind
½ cup coarsely chopped walnuts or pecans

Preheat oven to 350°F and place a rack at the middle level. Butter and flour a pan 8 x 8 x 2 inches; shake out the excess flour. Sift the flour before measuring and resift it with the baking powder, salt and cinnamon; set it aside. Scrub the zucchini and trim the ends, but do not peel them. Coarsely grate the zucchini with the shredding disk of a food processor or the largest holes of a 4-sided grater. Let shreds drain on paper towels. Cream the butter with the sugar and beat in the eggs until the mixture is soft and fluffy. Add the vanilla or lemon rind and fold in the zucchini. Add the sifted dry ingredients, blending until just incorporated. Fold in the nuts and turn the batter into the prepared pan.

Bake in the preheated oven for 45 to 50 minutes, or until a cake tester inserted in the center comes out clean. Cool in the pan on a rack for about 10 minutes. Remove from the pan and let cool completely on the rack. Cut into 2-inch squares or into bars 1 x 2 inches.

YIELD: 16 squares or 32 bars

Christmas and Holiday Cookies

Christmas Almond Wafers

These delicious wafers are German in origin (Mandelplattchen).

3 cups sifted all-purpose flour
½ pound (2 sticks) unsalted butter
1 cup granulated sugar
2 whole eggs
1 extra egg yolk
1 teaspoon grated lemon rind
Pinch of salt

½ teaspoon rosewater *or* ¼ teaspoon vanilla or almond extract
½ pound finely ground blanched almonds (2 cups)
1 egg yolk beaten with 2 Tablespoons milk for glaze

Sift the flour before measuring it. Cream the butter until light. Gradually add the sugar and beat until light and fluffy. Add the whole eggs and the yolk one at a time, beating after each addition. Blend in the lemon rind, salt and rosewater. Add the almonds, then beat in the flour until it is just incorporated. Chill the dough for about 1 hour until it will roll out easily.

Preheat oven to 375°F., and adjust the racks to divide the oven into thirds. Roll the dough out on a floured pastry cloth or between 2 sheets of wax paper to ⅛-inch thickness. Cut the dough into varying shapes and brush the tops with the egg yolk and milk glaze. Bake for 15 to 18 minutes, or until the cookies are lightly browned. After about 10 minutes, reverse the baking sheets from the upper to the lower racks and turn them from front to back. Transfer to a rack to cool.

YIELD: about 48 cookies

Christmas Cherries

Another favorite for the holiday festivities.

1 cup sifted flour	1½ teaspoons grated lemon rind
¼ teaspoon salt	½ teaspoon vanilla extract
¼ pound (1 stick) unsalted butter	¾ cup chopped nuts (see Note)
¼ cup granulated sugar	6 glacé cherries, cut into small
1 egg, separated	pieces
1 Tablespoon grated orange rind	

Sift the flour before measuring it and resift it with the salt. Cream the butter. Gradually add the sugar, and beat until the mixture is light. Separate the egg, reserving the white, and beat the yolk lightly. Add the beaten yolk, the orange and lemon rinds and the vanilla to the butter and sugar and beat until the mixture is very fluffy and light. Gradually stir in the flour and blend until just incorporated. Chill the dough for about 1 hour, or until it is easy to handle. It can be wrapped and kept overnight in the refrigerator.

Preheat oven to 350°F., and adjust the racks to divide the oven into thirds. Butter 2 cookie sheets, or line them with foil. Spread the chopped nuts out on wax paper. Beat the reserved egg white briefly until it is barely foamy. Using level teaspoon portions, roll pieces of the dough between your hands, forming balls a bit smaller than 1 inch in diameter. Roll the balls in the egg white, then in the chopped nuts. Press a piece of cherry into each. Place the balls about 1½ inches apart on the cookie sheets. Bake them for about 10 minutes. After about 6 minutes, reverse the sheets from the upper to the lower racks and turn them front to back. Cookies should be delicately colored. Transfer to a rack to cool.

YIELD: 36 cookies
NOTE: Before pistachios became so terribly expensive they looked wonderfully festive with their green color against the red of the cherry; for a less expensive choice, almonds, walnuts or pecans are fine.

Christmas Fruit Squares

Traditional holiday favorites, the fruit and nuts give them an old-fashioned flavor.

¾ cup sifted all-purpose flour
1½ teaspoons baking powder
1 teaspoon salt
3 Tablespoons unsalted butter
2 eggs

1 cup sifted confectioners' sugar
1 cup cut-up pitted dates
1 cup coarsely chopped pecans,
  walnuts or almonds
¾ cup mixed candied fruits

Frosting

½ cup sifted confectioners'
  sugar
1 Tablespoon unsalted butter,
  melted

1 teaspoon lemon juice

Preheat oven to 325°F., and adjust the rack to the middle level. Butter and flour a pan 9 x 9 x 2 inches; shake out excess flour. Sift the flour before measuring and resift it with the baking powder and salt. Melt the 3 tablespoons butter over low heat and set it aside to cool slightly. Beat the eggs until foamy and gradually beat in 1 cup sugar. Stir in the melted butter, and gradually add the sifted dry ingredients, mixing well. Add the dates, nuts and candied fruits. Spread the batter evenly in the prepared pan.

Bake for 30 to 35 minutes; the top will be light brown and slightly crusty. While the cake is still warm, spread it with a frosting made of ½ cup confectioners' sugar, 1 tablespoon melted butter and the lemon juice. Allow the cake to cool in the pan before cutting it with a thin sharp knife.

YIELD: 16 squares, 2-inch size

Christmas Wreath I

These traditional Christmas cookies are sometimes called Berliner Kranser *or* Eier Kringel. *They may, however, be of Danish rather than German origin. Made with egg yolks only, they would be good to make along with meringues or Cinnamon Stars (see p. 183), thereby balancing out the eggs.*

3 cups sifted cake flour
¼ teaspoon salt
½ pound (2 sticks) unsalted butter
½ cup granulated sugar
2 raw egg yolks

1 teaspoon vanilla extract, *or*
  ½ teaspoon vanilla extract and
  ½ teaspoon almond extract
2 hard-cooked egg yolks
1 egg white, lightly beaten
Colored sugar, or other toppings

Sift the flour before measuring and resift it with the salt. Set it aside. Cream the butter. Add the sugar and beat until the mixture is soft and fluffy. Beat in the raw egg yolks and the vanilla. Force the hard-cooked egg yolks through a sieve into the mixing bowl. Gradually add the flour, scraping the bowl to blend everything thoroughly. The dough should be smooth and soft. Chill the dough until it is firm enough to work and refrigerate it again if it starts to soften.

Preheat oven to 350°F., and adjust the racks to divide the oven into thirds. Butter 2 cookie sheets, or line them with foil, and set them aside. Form the wreaths in any of the following ways:

1. Using a pastry bag fitted with a rosette tube, pipe out the dough into a circle.

2. Roll out the dough on a floured pastry cloth or between 2 sheets of wax paper to ¼-inch thickness. Use a doughnut cutter or 2 cutters of different diameters to form the wreath shape. Use the leftover centers to make small round cookies.

3. Divide the dough into pieces and roll it with your hands into a rope shape about ⅜ inch in diameter. Cut the rope into 4-inch lengths and form each into a circle, joining the ends.

Brush each wreath with lightly beaten egg white and sprinkle with colored sugar or crystal sugar. If you have neither of those, crush some cubes of sugar and sprinkle with slivers of candied red cherries. For a variation, sprinkle some of the wreaths with ground almonds or walnuts or pecans. Bake on the prepared cookie sheets for 12 to 15 minutes. About halfway through baking time, reverse the cookie sheets from the upper to the lower rack and turn them from front to back.

YIELD: 72 wreaths, 1½ inches in diameter, or 27 wreaths, 2-inch size, and 27 rounds about 1-inch size
VARIATION: Add 1 teaspoon grated lemon rind and substitute lemon extract for the vanilla extract.

Christmas Wreath II

Richer tasting than Christmas Wreath I, these are a Swedish version of that perennial favorite.

4 cups sifted all-purpose flour
1 pound (4 sticks) unsalted butter
1 cup granulated sugar
4 raw egg yolks
1 teaspoon vanilla extract

1 teaspoon almond extract
4 hard-cooked egg yolks
2 egg whites, lightly beaten
Crushed lump sugar or crystal
  sugar (see Sources, p. 224)

Sift the flour before measuring it. Cream the butter until soft and light. Gradually add the sugar and beat until the mixture is very fluffy. Beat in the raw egg yolks and the vanilla and almond extracts. Force the hard-cooked yolks through a fine strainer into the mixing bowl. Mix briefly. Gradualy add the flour, scraping the bowl to blend everything thoroughly. You should have a smooth dough that is very soft. Chill the dough until it is firm enough to work. Refrigerate it again if it softens too much as you are working on it.

Preheat oven to 350°F., and adjust the racks to divide the oven into thirds. Butter 2 cookie sheets, or line them with foil. Form the cookies and decorate them as described in Christmas Wreath I. Bake them for about 12 minutes. After about 8 minutes, reverse the cookie sheets from the upper to the lower racks and turn them from front to back. Cookies are done when they are a very delicate brown. Transfer them to a rack to cool.

YIELD: 36 wreaths, 2-inch size, and 36 rounds, 1-inch size

Cinnamon Stars and Moons

One of the favorite Christmas cookies; these require an electric mixer, or the strength of a robot, because the egg white and sugar mixture should be beaten for at least 20 minutes (some recipes specify 30 to 45 minutes!).

4 egg whites (½ cup)
⅛ teaspoon salt
⅛ teaspoon cream of tartar
3 cups confectioners' sugar
1 teaspoon ground cinnamon

Grated rind of 1 lemon
¾ pound ground unblanched
  almonds (about 3 cups)
1 to 1½ cups confectioners' or
  granulated sugar

Be sure the egg whites are at room temperature. Beat the egg whites with the salt until they start to become foamy. Add the cream of tartar and continue beating until the whites are stiff but not dry. Gradually add the confectioners' sugar and beat for at least 20 minutes. The whites will be stiff and satiny. Remove ¼ cup of the meringue for topping and set aside. Add the cinnamon and lemon rind to the meringue and then fold in the almonds. Scrape the mixture out onto a large sheet of wax paper, wrap it, and refrigerate it for at least 3 hours, or preferably overnight.

Preheat oven to 325°F., and adjust the racks to divide the oven into thirds. When forming the cookies, remove about one quarter of the dough and refrigerate the part you are not working with. Sprinkle a heavy layer of confectioners' or granulated sugar on the work surface and pat or roll the dough to ⅜-inch thickness, turning it to coat both sides with sugar. Dip the cookie cutter into sugar frequently to prevent it sticking, and cut out small stars, crescents and rounds. Brush the top of each cookie with some of the reserved meringue.

Transfer the cookie to a greased baking sheet and bake for about 20 minutes, if you want them quite chewy, or up to 30 minutes if you want a crisp cookie with a chewy center.

YIELD: about 72 assorted shapes, or 100 stars, 1⅛-inch size

Dutch Speculaas

Sometimes called speculos *or* speculatius, *the name refers to the old wooden cookie molds that were used to form cookies in many shapes, some of them very large.*

2¼ cups sifted all-purpose flour
¼ teaspoon baking powder
¼ teaspoon salt
1½ teaspoons ground cinnamon
½ teaspoon ground nutmeg
½ teaspoon ground cloves
⅛ teaspoon white pepper
¼ teaspoon ground aniseed

¼ pound (1 stick) unsalted butter
1 cup firmly packed dark brown
  sugar
½ teaspoon grated lemon rind
3 to 5 Tablespoons milk
1/3 cup slivered blanched almonds

Sift the flour before measuring it and resift it with the baking powder, salt, spices and aniseed. Cream the butter until light. Gradually add the sugar and beat until the mixture is light and fluffy. Beat in the lemon rind and gradually add the flour mixture. The dough will be very stiff. Gradually add the milk, a little at a time. If you are going to roll out the dough, it should be slightly soft. If you are going to press the dough into a mold, it should be stiffer. If you add too much milk, knead in a little more flour. Wrap the dough airtight and let it rest in the refrigerator overnight.

Preheat oven to 350°F., and adjust the racks to divide the oven into thirds. Butter and flour 2 baking sheets, or line them with foil. *For cut-out cookies*, roll the dough out on a lightly floured surface or between 2 sheets of wax paper to ¼-inch thickness. Transfer the cut-outs to the prepared baking sheets. Sprinkle almonds on top of cookies, pressing them in lightly. *For molded cookies*, flour the molds thoroughly and shake out excess flour. Roll the dough to ¼-inch thickness, wrap it around the rolling pin, and lay it over the mold. Press the dough in with your fingers. Trim the excess or remove it with your fingers, and unmold dough onto a lightly floured work surface. With a sharp knife or a pastry wheel, cut between the designs and transfer them to the cookie sheet. Reflour the mold as necessary.

Bake for 12 to 16 minutes, or until the edges are light brown; possibly 18 to 20 minutes if you have used a deep mold. About three quarters through the estimated baking time, reverse the baking sheets from the upper to the lower racks and turn them from front to back. Transfer the cookies to a rack to dry.

YIELD: about 45 squares, 2-inch size

Pfeffernüsse

German in origin (translation — pepper nuts), these cookies should be stored for several days before baking and for a week or two before serving.

3 cups sifted all-purpose flour
1 teaspoon ground cinnamon
½ teaspoon ground cloves
¼ teaspoon ground cardamon
¼ teaspoon finely ground pepper
   (preferably white)
3 eggs

1 cup granulated sugar
1½ ounces blanched almonds,
   finely ground (1/3 cup)
1/3 cup finely chopped mixed
   citron and candied orange peel
1 teaspoon grated lemon rind
Confectioners' sugar

Sift the flour before measuring and resift it with the spices. Beat the eggs until they are frothy. Gradually add the sugar, and continue beating until thick and lemon-colored. Slowly mix in the flour and finally the almonds, fruit peels and lemon rind. Wrap the dough airtight in foil and refrigerate for 2 or 3 days.

Preheat oven to 325°F., and adjust the racks to divide the oven into thirds. Butter 2 baking sheets, or line them with foil. Work with about a third of the dough at a time and keep the rest chilled. Roll out the dough on a floured pastry cloth or between 2 sheets of wax paper to about ⅜-inch thickness. Cut with a round cookie cutter. Place 1 inch apart on the prepared baking sheets. Bake for 15 to 18 minutes, or until light brown. Transfer to a rack to cool. Store with half an apple in an airtight container for 1 to 2 weeks before serving. Dust with confectioners' sugar when serving.

YIELD: about 85 rounds, 1-inch size
VARIATION: The dough can be formed into logs when firm enough to handle, to be refrigerated and sliced into rounds.

Russian Tea Cakes

A holiday favorite; these keep very well.

2¼ cups sifted all-purpose flour   1 teaspoon vanilla extract
½ pound (2 sticks) unsalted butter   ¾ cup chopped pecans or walnuts
½ cup sifted confectioners' sugar   Confectioners' sugar

Preheat oven to 350°F., and adjust the racks to divide the oven into thirds. Butter 2 cookie sheets, or line them with foil. Sift the flour before measuring. Cream the butter. Add the confectioners' sugar, and beat until mixture is light and fluffy. Add the vanilla. Gradually add the sifted flour and beat until it is just incorporated. Fold in the nuts. By rounded teaspoons, form the dough into balls, flouring your hands lightly to prevent sticking. Place the balls 1 inch apart on the cookie sheets.

Bake for 12 to 14 minutes. After about 8 minutes, reverse the cookie sheets from the upper to the lower racks and turn them from front to back. Cookies will be light gold in color. While they are still warm, roll them in confectioners' sugar and cool them on a rack. Roll them again in confectioners' sugar after they are cool.

YIELD: 40 cookies

Yugoslavian Christmas Squares

This is a festive-looking cookie with a meringue topping over currant jelly.

2 cups sifted all-purpose flour
½ pound (2 sticks) unsalted butter
1½ cups granulated sugar
1 egg yolk
¼ teaspoon salt
1 cup currant jelly
4 egg whites

¼ teaspoon cream of tartar
¾ cup shelled walnuts, finely ground
1 teaspoon vanilla extract
1 cup shelled walnuts, coarsely chopped

Preheat oven to 325°F., and adjust a rack to the middle level. Butter a pan 9 x 9 x 2 inches. Sift the flour before measuring. Cream the butter until soft. Add ½ cup of the sugar and beat until mixture is light and fluffy. Beat in the egg yolk and salt. Stir in the flour and blend it in thoroughly. Pat this mixture into an even layer in the bottom of the prepared pan. Beat the jelly to make it more spreadable, and cover the dough with an even layer of jelly. Beat the egg whites until foamy and add the cream of tartar. Continue beating until stiff but not dry. Gradually add the remaining cup of sugar, beating at the same time. Add the vanilla and fold in the *finely ground* nuts. Spread the meringue over the jelly and sprinkle on the *coarsely chopped* nuts.

Bake for about 40 minutes, until the meringue is browned. Cool in the pan, on a rack, before cutting into 1½-inch squares.

YIELD: 36 squares, 1½-inch size

Basler Leckerli (Swiss Honey Drops)

This is a traditional Christmas cookie. Like some other old recipes, the dough is mixed and then rests at room temperature for 2 days before baking. The honey in these cookies gives them their long-lasting quality. After baking, they should be stored in an airtight box for 2 or 3 weeks to ripen before being served. When stored properly, these will keep well for months.

½ cup honey
1 cup sugar
1/3 cup each of candied orange and
    lemon peel, *or* 2/3 cup orange
    peel, finely chopped
1 teaspoon grated lemon rind
2 Tablespoons kirsch liqueur
    (Optional)

1 cup sliced blanched almonds
2¼ cups sifted all-purpose flour
1 teaspoon ground cinnamon
1 teaspoon ground nutmeg
½ teaspoon ground cloves
1 teaspoon baking soda
¼ cup water

In a heavy saucepan cook the honey and ½ cup of the sugar over low heat. Stir until the mixture boils; remove from heat. Add the candied orange and lemon peels and the grated lemon rind. Stir in the kirsch if you use it; let mixture cool to lukewarm and add the almonds. Sift the flour before measuring and resift it with the spices and baking soda. Stir the flour and spices into the cooled honey mixture. Transfer dough to a bowl, cover it, and let it stand at cool room temperature for at least 2 days.

Preheat oven to 325°F., and adjust the racks to divide the oven into thirds. Butter and flour 2 cookie sheets. Roll out the dough on a well-floured pastry cloth or other floured surface, to about ¼- or ⅜-inch thickness. Cut the dough into bars 1½ x 3 inches, or form them with special *leckerli* or *springerle* molds. Bake for about 25 minutes, or until lightly browned. Transfer to wax paper.

Cook remaining ½ cup of sugar with the water until it reaches 230°F. on a candy thermometer, or thread stage (slightly cooled, it will spin a thread when rubbed between thumb and forefinger). Brush each bar or cookie with the hot syrup. Transfer to a rack to cool. When completely cool, store in an airtight container.

YIELD: about 50 bars

Kourabiedes

These delectable and buttery cookies are an adaptation of a Greek holiday cookie, sometimes called Kurabia in Armenian cookbooks. Some recipes include ground almonds, others do not. The liqueur usually called for is the anise-flavored ouzo, or Greek brandy. Other versions use sherry, orange juice, etc.

2½ cups sifted all-purpose flour
½ teaspoon baking powder
½ cup confectioners' sugar
4 ounces blanched almonds
½ pound (2 sticks) unsalted butter,
   clarified and chilled (see Note)

1 egg yolk
¼ cup liqueur (Grand Marnier,
   brandy, etc.), *or* 2 Tablespoons
   brandy and 2 Tablespoons orange
   juice, *or* ¼ cup orange juice

Sift the flour before measuring. Resift it with the baking powder and set it aside. After measuring the confectioners' sugar, sift it and set it aside. In a food processor, blender or nut grinder, grind the almonds to about the consistency of sea salt or kosher salt and set them aside. In the bowl of an electric mixer (or in a mixing bowl using a hand-held electric mixer) cream the butter until it is very soft and fluffy. Add the sugar gradually, beating until the mixture is almost like whipped cream. Add the egg yolk and liqueur (or orange juice), blending them in thoroughly. Gradually add the flour, scraping the bowl to blend it in thoroughly; then add the nuts. Turn the dough out onto a lightly floured surface and knead it lightly, adding more flour if necessary, until the dough is smooth. Wrap it in wax paper and chill it until it is firm.

Preheat oven to 350°F., and adjust the racks to divide the oven into thirds. To form the cookies, roll the dough out on a floured pastry cloth or between 2 sheets of wax paper to ¼-inch thickness. With a cookie cutter, cut the dough into the traditional crescent shapes, or any other shape you prefer, and place them close to each other, but not touching, on an ungreased cookie sheet. Alternatively you can roll the dough into a log about 2 inches in diameter and slice it into ¼-inch rounds. You can also form the log into a crescent-shaped roll (see p. 26) and slice it into ¼-inch crescents.

Bake for about 12 minutes, or until cookies are delicately colored. Halfway through the baking time, reverse the cookie sheets from front to back and from lower to upper racks. Remove from sheets and cool on a rack. The cookies are very often served with a dusting of confectioners' sugar. I think the delicate flavor comes through better without the additional sugar.

YIELD: 72 crescent-shape cookies, or 48 round cookies, 2-inch size
NOTE: The cookies can be made without clarifying the butter of course, but the delicate texture that results from using clarified butter is well worth the time involved.

Lebkuchen

A German Christmas cookie, made with honey as so many traditional cookies were, mostly because honey was available and not as expensive as sugar for the farmers' wives. This dough should be stored overnight before being baked, and finished cakes should be allowed to mellow for 2 to 3 weeks before being served; the cookies will keep for ages.

1 cup honey
¾ cup firmly packed dark brown
   sugar
1 Tablespoon lemon juice
1 teaspoon grated lemon rind
1 egg, beaten
1/3 cup finely chopped mixed
   candied orange peel and citron

1/3 cup finely chopped blanched
   almonds
2¾ cups sifted all-purpose flour
½ teaspoon baking soda
1 teaspoon ground cinnamon
½ teaspoon ground cloves
½ teaspoon ground allspice
½ teaspoon ground nutmeg

Frosting

1 cup sifted confectioners' sugar
4 to 5 teaspoons water

In a heavy saucepan, large enough for mixing the dough, bring the honey and brown sugar to a boil over low heat, stirring. Remove from heat and stir in the lemon juice and grated rind. Beat in the egg. Cool the mixture slightly and add the candied fruits and the almonds. Sift the flour before measuring and resift it with the baking soda and all the spices. Add flour to the saucepan, stirring well to mix it in thoroughly. Transfer dough to a bowl and refrigerate it overnight.

Preheat oven to 400°F., and adjust the racks to divide the oven into thirds. Butter and flour 2 cookie sheets and shake off excess flour, or line them with foil. Work with one third of the dough at a time, keeping the rest refrigerated. Roll out the dough on a floured pastry cloth or between 2 sheets of wax paper to ¼-inch thickness. Cut the dough into shapes with cutters, or cut it into bars 1½ x 2½ inches. The dough is difficult to cut and you will have to flour the knife and cutters. Place the shaped cookies or bars 2 inches apart on the cookie sheets. An alternative way of forming the bars is to spread the dough on a greased and floured cookie sheet to a thickness of ¼ inch and cut it into bars after it is baked.

Bake for 8 to 10 minutes for individual shapes or for about 15 minutes if you bake the dough in one large sheet. The edges will be lightly browned and the top should spring back when pressed gently. Mix the confectioners' sugar and water and spread on the hot cookies or large sheet of dough. Transfer cookies to a rack to cool. Cut the large sheet of dough into bars after it is cool.

YIELD: about 48 cakes

Springerle

The word springerle *means "little horse" in a dialect of southern Germany. It is a traditional Christmas cookie whose roots are pagan in origin. In pre-Christian times the winter solstice was celebrated by the sacrifice of real animals or, very often, effigies of animals baked in dough.* Springerle *and other cut-out cookies have come to be associated with Christmas festivities. These cookies are not baked for 24 hours after molding and are best allowed to mellow for a week in an airtight container before being served. They are formed by rolling dough on a* springerle *board, or by rolling dough with a carved* springerle *rolling pin, or by pressing dough on individual blocks.*

4 cups sifted all-purpose flour
1 teaspoon baking powder
½ teaspoon salt
4 eggs

2 cups granulated sugar
Grated rind of 2 lemons
¼ cup whole aniseeds

Sift the flour with the baking powder and salt. Beat the eggs until they are very light and lemon colored. Gradually add the sugar, beating well with each addition until the mixture is very pale and thick. Stir in the lemon rind. Add the flour, beating just enough to blend it in. Turn the dough out onto wax paper and wrap it well; refrigerate for at least 2 hours.

Roll out the dough, one third at a time. Roll it slightly less than ½ inch thick, keeping it as rectangular as possible and about the width of the *springerle* rolling pin or board. *If you are using a springerle board,* flour it lightly. Roll out the dough on the floured board to ¼- to ⅜-inch thickness and invert it on a lightly floured surface. *If using a springerle rolling pin,* flour pin lightly and roll it over the dough *once only,* pressing firmly so that the dough is about ¼-inch thick and presssing evenly so the imprint is clear. *If using individual blocks,* roll the dough ¼-inch thick and press down firmly and evenly with the block. Cut along the dividing lines to separate the individual cookies, transfer to a lightly floured surface, and let cookies stand uncovered overnight.

Preheat oven to 325°F., and adjust the racks to divide the oven into thirds. Butter 2 cookie sheets and sprinkle them with aniseeds. Transfer the cut designs onto the sheets. Bake for 14 to 18 minutes, until cookies are barely golden at the edges. Don't let them brown. Let them stand for 1 minute before transferring to racks to cool. When completely cool, store in an airtight container for a week to 10 days before serving.

YIELD: 60 cookies

Moravian Christmas Cut-Outs

The Moravian sect founded Salem, North Carolina, in 1764. It was eventually surrounded by the city of Winston and became Winston-Salem. To avert the destruction of the historic settlement, a nonprofit organization called Old Salem, Inc., saved and restored Salem, calling it "Old Salem." Most unusual for its time, Salem was a completely planned town laid out in a precise grid by the church elders, who also regulated the commerical enterprises. Famous for its gingerbread, the settlement is also known for these cookies. They are rolled out paper thin and cut in fancy shapes; the cookie cutters were made by the local tinsmith.

1 cup molasses	1 teaspoon baking soda
2/3 cup firmly packed dark brown sugar	1½ teaspoons ground ginger
¾ cup unsalted butter (1½ sticks) or lard or half of each	1 teaspoon ground nutmeg or mace
4½ cups sifted all-purpose flour	1 teaspoon ground cinnamon
½ teaspoon salt	½ teaspoon ground cloves
	1/3 cup water

In a heavy 2- or 3-quart saucepan, combine the molasses, brown sugar and butter or lard. Bring just to the boil, remove from heat, and allow to cool slightly. Sift the flour before measuring and resift it with the salt, baking soda and spices. Add this to the saucepan, stirring it in. Add the water and combine all into a dough. Wrap the dough and chill it for about 6 hours, or overnight.

Preheat oven to 375°F., and adjust the racks to divide the oven into thirds. Butter 2 cookie sheets, or line them with foil. Working with one fourth of the dough at a time, roll it out as thin as possible, less than ⅛-inch thick. Cut shapes with lightly floured cookie cutters, and place them 1½ inches apart on the prepared cookie sheets. Bake for 8 to 10 minutes, until lightly browned. After about 5 minutes, reverse the sheets from the upper to the lower rack and turn them from front to back. Cool the cookies on the sheets for about 2 minutes, then transfer them to a rack to cool.

YIELD: 60 cookies

Spritz Cookies

A Christmas classic from Scandinavia, these are traditionally made in small fancy shapes and decorated with frosting, colored sugar, chocolate sprinkles, chopped toasted nuts, sliced nuts, flaked coconut, minced candied cherries or other fruits.

2¼ cups sifted all-purpose flour
½ teaspoon salt
½ pound (2 sticks) unsalted butter
2/3 cup sugar

2 egg yolks, lightly beaten
1 teaspoon vanilla extract,
  or ½ teaspoon almond extract

Preheat oven to 375°F., and adjust the racks to divide the oven into thirds. Sift the flour before measuring and resift it with the salt. Cream the butter until soft. Beat in the sugar until light and fluffy. Add the egg yolks and vanilla or almond extract, beating well. Add the flour gradually, blending it in well. Form the dough into various shapes, using a pastry bag or cookie press, and place about 1 inch apart on ungreased or foil-lined cookie sheets.

Bake for 7 to 10 minutes, until lightly colored and almost firm, not brown. After about 5 minutes, reverse the cookie sheets from the upper to the lower racks and turn them from front to back. Let them stand on the baking sheets for 2 or 3 minutes before transferring them to a rack to cool.

YIELD: about 60 cookies
NOTE: If you have lined the cookie sheets with foil, slide the foil with the cookies on it off the sheet and let them stand on the foil for 2 or 3 minutes before transferring to a rack to cool.

Spritz Almond Cookies

On the theory that one can't have too much of a good thing, here's another equally delicious version of the Christmas Spritz.

2 cups sifted all-purpose flour
½ teaspoon salt
½ pound (2 sticks) unsalted butter
½ cup confectioners' sugar
2 egg yolks, lightly beaten

1 teaspoon almond extract
2 ounces blanched almonds,
   (½ cup) very finely ground
2 Tablespoons brandy or rum

Preheat oven to 375°F., and adjust the racks to divide the oven into thirds. Sift the flour before measuring and resift it with the salt. Cream the butter until soft. Beat in the sugar until light and fluffy. Add the egg yolks, beating them in, and the almond extract. Stir in the ground almonds. Gradually add the sifted flour and salt, mixing it in well. Stir in the brandy or rum. Form the dough into various shapes, using either a pastry bag or cookie press, and place them about 1 inch apart on ungreased or foil-lined cookie sheets.

Bake for 7 to 10 minutes, until lightly colored and almost firm. After about 5 minutes, reverse the sheets from the upper to the lower rack and turn them from front to back. Let them stand on the baking sheets for 2 or 3 minutes before transferring to a rack to cool.

YIELD: about 48 cookies
NOTE: See Note on Spritz I.

Spritz White Cookies

Still another version of Spritz, but this one uses only egg whites so it cleverly balances with either of the other two, which use yolks. Bake all three and try to decide which you like best!

2¼ cups sifted all-purpose flour
¼ teaspoon salt
½ pound (2 sticks) unsalted butter

2/3 cup granulated sugar
3 egg whites
1 teaspoon vanilla extract

Preheat the oven to 375°F., and adjust the racks to divide the oven into thirds. Butter 2 cookie sheets, or line them with foil. Sift the flour before measuring and resift it with the salt. Cream the butter until light and fluffy. Add the egg whites, beating them in well, and the vanilla. Add the sifted flour and salt. Form the dough into various shapes, using either a pastry bag or cookie press, and place them about 1 inch apart on ungreased or foil-lined cookie sheets.

Bake for 7 to 10 minutes, until lightly colored and almost firm, not brown. After about 5 minutes, reverse the sheets from the upper to the lower rack and turn them from front to back. Let them stand on the baking sheets for 2 or 3 minutes before transferring to a rack to cool.

YIELD: about 60 cookies
NOTE: See Note on Spritz I.

Crackers

Anise Toast

These are Italian in origin but are similar in texture to the Dutch Zwieback and French biscotte. Essentially it is a dough that is baked in loaf form, then sliced and toasted until pale gold in color. This makes the toast crisp and long-lasting. Europeans start their lifelong attachment to them as babies when the toast is given to them while they are teething. In adult life they are usually accompanied by coffee or wine.

2 eggs
½ cup plus 2 Tablespoons sugar
1 ¼ cups sifted cake flour

Scant ¼ teaspoon anise extract, *or* 4 drops of anise oil (see Note)
1 teaspoon aniseeds

Cream the eggs and sugar until very fluffy and almost white (about 5 minutes in an electric mixer). Add the flour gradually, then the extract and seeds. Preheat oven to 375°F. Butter and flour a small loaf pan, 4 to 5 inches wide. Scrape the dough into the loaf pan, smoothing it gently to level it. Bake in the middle level of the preheated oven for about 20 minutes. The loaf should be delicately colored. When done, remove the loaf from the pan but leave the oven on.

Let the loaf cool briefly, then slice it about ½ inch or 3/8 inch thick. Place the slices on an ungreased cookie sheet and toast them in the oven, turning them once, for about 5 minutes on each side. Transfer to a rack to cool before storing.

YIELD: 16 half-inch toasts
VARIATION: Some recipes call for sprinkling the warm toast with a few drops of anisette liqueur, then letting them cool for storage.
NOTE: A standard 6-cup loaf pan measuring 8½ by 4½ inches is fine. The dough does not fill the pan but it doesn't matter.

Anise oil, technically called Oil of Anethol, is the basis for anise extract and is available at specialty stores (see Sources, p. 224).

Lena's Almond Biscotti

This is really a rusk, rather than a cookie. Like that other Italian delicacy, anise toast, these are baked in loaf form and then sliced and rebaked briefly. My dear friend Lena learned to make these from her Italian mother. They are dry and crunchy. I prefer them with the lesser amount of sugar as they are not supposed to be really sweet. They become drier with age, if they last that long, and are often dunked into coffee or wine.

2½ cups sifted all-purpose flour
1½ teaspoons baking powder
¼ teaspoon salt
3 eggs
1 to 1 1/3 cups granulated sugar

½ teaspoon almond extract, *or*
  2 teaspoons almond liqueur
½ pound blanched almonds,
  slivered (2 cups)

Preheat oven to 350°F., and place a rack at the middle level. Butter and flour a baking sheet 12 x 16 inches and shake off the excess flour, or line sheet with foil. If your baking sheets are smaller than 12 x 16, adjust the racks to divide the oven into thirds and use 2 sheets. Sift the flour before measuring and resift it with the baking powder and salt. Beat the eggs with 1 cup sugar, or use the larger amount if you prefer, until thick and very pale, about 10 minutes with an electric mixer, 20 by hand. The mixture should form a ribbon when the beater is lifted. Beat in the almond extract or liqueur. Gradually add the sifted dry ingredients, beating until just incorporated and smooth. Fold in the almonds.

Use a large spoon and a spatula to place mounds of dough lengthwise on the baking sheet, the mounds touching each other to form a continuous strip about 13 inches long and about 3 inches wide. Try to keep the strip even but don't smooth the top or sides with the spatula. If you feel it is too uneven, shape the sides very gently with wet hands. The strip will smooth out in baking. Form a second strip of dough in the same way; allow about 4 inches of space between the strips. Bake for about 25 minutes, until firm to the touch and lightly colored.

Remove the baking sheet from the oven but don't turn the oven off. If you used foil, slide the foil liner off the sheet and let the 2 strips stand on the foil for about 10 minutes. Carefully peel the foil off the back of the strips and transfer strips to a board for slicing. If you used a buttered and floured sheet, let it stand for about 10 minutes before sliding the strips onto the cutting board. With a sharp knife, preferably a serrated one, cut the strips into slices about 3¾ inch thick. Place the slices on the baking sheet (not necessary to use foil liner for this step), allowing as much space between slices as possible. Return the sheet to the oven for about 10 minutes. Remove and let the slices cool on a rack.

YIELD: 36 biscotti
VARIATION: Use hazelnuts instead of almonds.

Caraway Rye Crackers

A crisp cracker which goes well with soups or predinner drinks.

1 cup sifted all-purpose flour
1 cup sifted rye flour
½ teaspoon salt
1 Tablespoon caraway seeds
3 ounces (¾ stick) chilled unsalted
  butter, cut into small bits

2 Tablespoons chilled vegetable
  shortening, cut into small bits
3 to 5 Tablespoons ice water
1 egg white, beaten (optional)

Put the flours, salt and seeds into a mixing bowl or the work bowl of a food processor and mix them briefly. As if you were making pastry, cut the bits of butter and vegetable shortening into the flour until the mixture resembles coarse meal. Add 3 tablespoons of the ice water and work it quickly until the dough forms a ball, adding more water if necessary. If you are using a food processor, do not let the dough form a ball but stop the machine when the dough starts to cohere and before it has reached the ball stage. Divide the dough into 2 parts and wrap and refrigerate them for at least 2 hours. The dough can also be formed into 2 round logs, to be chilled and then sliced into ⅛ -inch rounds.

Preheat oven to 350°F., and adjust the racks to divide the oven into thirds. Butter 2 cookie sheets, or line them with unbuttered foil. Roll the chilled dough out on a lightly floured surface or between 2 sheets of wax paper to ⅛ -inch thickness. Cut the dough into rounds or squares. Transfer to the cookie sheets. If you like, brush the tops with beaten egg white. Bake for 8 to 10 minutes, until crackers are crisp and golden brown. Transfer to a rack to cool.

YIELD: 60 crackers
NOTE: You can roll the dough right on the cookie sheet, forming a rectangle, and cut it with a pastry wheel into squares or rectangles.

Cornmeal Crackers

This is a slightly dry cracker, with a grainy consistency due to the cornmeal. They are only slighly "hot" with a tablespoon of chili powder, so adjust the seasoning to your taste.

1 1/3 cups sifted all-purpose flour	½ teaspoon baking powder
1 cup yellow cornmeal	3 ounces (¾ stick) unsalted butter
½ teaspoon salt	2 eggs, lightly beaten with
1 to 1 ½ Tablespoons chili powder	1 teaspoon water

Preheat oven to 400°F., and adjust the racks to divide the oven into thirds. Lightly butter 2 cookie sheets and set them aside. Sift together the flour, cornmeal, salt, chili powder and baking powder and put the mixture into a mixing bowl or the work bowl of a food processor along with any particles remaining in the sifter. Cut the butter into bits and work it into the flour and cornmeal mixture. Add the eggs and, if necessary, more water. The dough should be quite stiff. Roll the dough out on a lightly floured surface with a floured rolling pin, or roll it between 2 sheets of wax paper, to ¼-inch thickness. Cut the dough into 2-inch rounds with a cookie cutter and place the rounds on buttered cookie sheets. Bake for 12 to 15 minutes, until the edges are lightly browned. Transfer to a rack to cool.

YIELD: 40 crackers

Cornell Crackers

The nutritious bread devised at Cornell University contained soy flour, wheat germ and nonfat dry milk. This buttery salty cracker is based on the same ingredients.

¼ pound (1 stick) unsalted butter, softened
½ cup hot water
2 cups *un*sifted all-purpose flour
3 Tablespoons *un*sifted soy flour

3 Tablespoons nonfat dry milk powder
3 Tablespoons wheat germ (optional)
1 Tablespoon sugar
2 teaspoons salt

Cut the butter into 4 or 5 pieces and place it in a mixing bowl. Pour the hot water over the butter and set it aside to cool slightly. Measure the flour by scooping a 1-cup measure into the flour and leveling it off with a spatula or knife. Combine and sift together 1 cup of the all-purpose flour with the soy flour and nonfat dry milk powder. Stir in the wheat germ if you use it. Beat the water and butter lightly; then stir in combined flour, soy flour and dry milk. Stir in the sugar and salt; blend thoroughly. Gradually add the rest of the flour, forming a ball of dough. Turn the dough out on a lightly floured work surface and knead it briefly until smooth. Add a bit more flour if necessary to give it firmness, but be cautious about adding more flour. Wrap the dough in plastic wrap and let it rest at room temperature for about 1 hour.

Preheat oven to 400°F., and adjust the racks to divide the oven into thirds. Divide the dough into halves; keep one half covered and roll the other one out into a thin rectangle, ⅛ inch thick, about 8 x 10 inches. Using a pastry wheel, preferably one with a crimped edge, cut the dough into squares or rectangles. Transfer them to an unbuttered or foil-lined cookie sheet, placing them ½ inch apart. Roll out and cut the other half of the dough.

Bake for 15 to 20 minutes, until lightly browned with slightly darker edges. After about 8 minutes, reverse the cookie sheets from the upper to the lower racks and turn them from front. to back. If at the end of the baking time some crackers are still soft to the touch, remove those that are done and give the others a few more minutes, but check them!

YIELD: 40 squares, 2-inch size, or 80 rectangles, 1 x 2 inches

Oatmeal Wheat Crackers

A nonsweet oatmeal cracker as nutritious as it is delicious

¾ cup sifted all-purpose flour
¼ cup sifted whole-wheat flour
¼ cup wheat germ
2 cups rolled oats, preferably
  quick cooking
1 teaspoon salt

3 ounces (¾ stick) unsalted butter
3 Tablespoons honey
½ cup water
1 egg white, lightly beaten
2 Tablespoons toasted
  sesame seeds (optional)

Sift both flours before measuring and place them in a work bowl. Stir in the wheat germ, oats and salt. Place the butter, honey and water in a small saucepan and place over low heat, stirring, until the butter has melted. Pour this mixture over the flour and oats in the bowl and stir until dough forms a ball and pulls away from the sides of the bowl. Divide the dough into 2 portions, wrap each in wax paper, and refrigerate for about 1 hour.

Preheat oven to 350°F., and adjust the racks to divide the oven into thirds. Butter 2 cookie sheets, or line them with foil. Roll out half of the dough on a floured pastry cloth or between 2 sheets of wax paper to ⅛-inch thickness, rectangular in shape. Roll the dough loosely around your rolling pin and transfer it to a cookie sheet. If you have rolled dough between sheets of wax paper, remove the top sheet of wax paper and flip the dough over onto the cookie sheet. Remove the second piece of wax paper. Using a pastry wheel with a crimped edge or a pizza cutter or sharp knife, cut the dough into squares. Brush the tops with egg white, sprinkle lightly with sesame seeds, if you use them.

Bake for 15 to 20 minutes, or until lightly browned. After 10 to 12 minutes, reverse the cookie sheets from the upper to the lower racks and turn them from front to back. Transfer to a rack to cool.

YIELD: 48 crackers

Onion Cheese Crackers

These flavorful crackers are great served with soup, salad or predinner drinks. Easily made in a food processor.

¾ cup sifted all-purpose flour
2 Tablespoons sifted or *un*sifted soy flour
½ teaspoon salt
⅛ to ¼ teaspoon cayenne pepper
2 Tablespoons wheat germ

3¼ ounces (2/3 stick) unsalted butter, cut into bits
6 ounces sharp Cheddar cheese, grated (1½ cups)
3 Tablespoons minced onion

Sift the flour before measuring and resift it with the soy flour, salt and cayenne into a large bowl, or the work bowl of a food processor. Stir in wheat germ. Cut the butter into small pieces and work it into the flour. Blend in the cheese and the onion. Knead the dough very briefly. Form it into 2 logs, each about 1½ inches in diameter and about 7 inches long. Wrap in wax paper and refrigerate for several hours, until firm enough to slice. Do not attempt to freeze.

Preheat oven to 350°F., and adjust the racks to divide the oven into thirds. Butter 2 cookie sheets, or line them with foil. Remove dough from refrigerator. With a thin sharp knife, slice it into rounds ¼ inch thick. Place rounds about 1 inch apart on the prepared cookie sheets. Bake for 12 to 15 minutes, until lightly browned. After about 8 minutes, reverse the cookie sheets from the upper to the lower racks and turn them from front to back. Transfer to a rack to cool.

YIELD: 48 crackers

Peruvian Parmesan Pennies

The cheese that is used for these in Peru is not Parmesan but an Argentinian cheese that is similar. When I first tasted these many years ago in Lima, I asked my friend Helena for the recipe. She said is was just 100 grams of cheese, 100 grams of flour and 100 grams of butter. Not being familar with metric measurements at that time, I wasn't sure how to go about converting that to our system of measuring. Now having weighed everything on my trusty scale, here it is.

3½ ounces unsalted butter
   (1 stick less 1 Tablespoon)
¾ cup grated Parmesan cheese
¾ cup sifted all-purpose flour

¼ teaspoon salt
⅛ teaspoon cayenne pepper,
   or to taste

Cream the butter until soft, and blend with the cheese. Sift the flour before measuring and resift it with the salt and cayenne. Add the flour to the butter and cheese mixture, mixing in well. Place the dough on wax paper and form it into a log 1¾ to 2 inches in diameter. Chill for several hours or overnight until firm enough to slice.

Preheat oven to 350°F., and adjust the racks to divide the oven into thirds. Remove the chilled dough from the refrigerator, unwrap it, and slice it crosswise with a thin sharp knife. The slices should be about ⅛ inch thick. Place the rounds on unbuttered cookie sheets.

Bake pennies for 12 to 15 minutes, or until lightly colored. After 7 or 8 minutes, reverse the cookie sheets from the upper to the lower racks and turn them from front to back. Remove cookie sheets from the oven. Quickly loosen all the crackers with a metal spatula and transfer them to a rack to cool.

YIELD: 50 crackers
VARIATION: Before baking, sprinkle rounds with 2 Tablespoons caraway seeds or toasted sesame seeds.

Sesame Sticks

I have found that it's best to make a big batch of these as they seem to go very fast.

2 Tablespoons sesame seeds
3 cups sifted all-purpose flour
1½ teaspoons baking powder
1 teaspoon salt

6 ounces (1½ sticks) unsalted
  butter
1 egg, beaten with ½ cup milk
1 egg, beaten with 1 Tablespoon
  milk

Preheat oven to 375°F., and adjust the racks to divide the oven into thirds. Butter 2 cookie sheets and set them aside. Toast the sesame seeds in a heavy skillet, shaking and stirring until they are lightly browned. Remove them from pan and set aside to cool. Sift the flour before measuring and resift it with the baking powder and salt into your work bowl. Melt the butter over low heat and combine it with the egg beaten with the ½ cup of milk. Add this to the flour mixture and blend thoroughly. Turn the dough out on a work surface and knead it lightly. Roll the dough out on a floured board or between 2 sheets of wax paper into a ¼-inch-thick rectangle. With a pastry wheel, preferably one with a crimped edge, cut the dough into sticks 4 inches long by ½ inch wide. Transfer these to the cookie sheets. Beat the other egg with the tablespoon of milk and brush this glaze on the pastry sticks, using a goose feather or pastry brush. Sprinkle with sesame seeds.

Bake for 20 to 22 minutes, or until golden brown. About halfway through the baking time, reverse the cookie sheets from top to bottom and turn them from front to back. Remove from oven and transfer to a rack to cool.

YIELD: 96 sticks

Sesame Soy Crackers

These are thin and crisp with a slightly nutlike flavor. They're so good no one will realize how nutritious they are, thanks to the soy flour.

½ cup toasted sesame seeds
1 2/3 cups sifted all-purpose flour
1/3 cup sifted or *un*sifted soy flour
1 teaspoon baking powder

½ teaspoon salt
¼ pound (1 stick) unsalted butter,
   very cold, and cut into bits
1/3 cup milk

Preheat oven to 375°F., and adjust the racks to divide the oven into thirds. Toast the sesame seeds in a dry skillet over medium heat, shaking the pan so that they don't burn. When golden brown, remove them from the pan and set them aside to cool. Sift the flour before measuring and resift it with the soy flour, baking powder and salt. Place the sifted dry ingredients in a mixing bowl, or the work bowl of a food processor, and add the cut-up bits of cold butter unblended. Stir in the cooled sesame seeds. Add the milk and mix just until a soft dough is formed. If the dough is dry and crumbly, add 1 or 2 teaspoons of milk, 1 teaspoon at a time. Divide the dough into halves and form each into a flat round.

On a lightly floured surface, or floured pastry cloth, or between 2 sheets of wax paper, roll out half of the dough to ⅛-inch thickness. Cut into 2-inch rounds and place them ½ inch apart on an ungreased, or foil-lined, cookie sheet. Repeat with remaining dough. With the tines of a fork, prick each round 2 or 3 times. Bake for 8 or 9 minutes, until faintly colored; the centers will be slightly soft to the touch. After about 5 minutes, reverse the cookie sheets from the upper to the lower rack and turn them from front to back. Cool slightly on the sheets before transferring to racks.

YIELD: 60 rounds, 2-inch size

Sesame Wheat Crackers

These crackers have buttery sesame flavor that goes well with soups and drinks.
They are good also as a nonsweet snack. The dough will keep unbaked in the
freezer for months.

1/3 cup sesame seeds
1 cup unbleached flour
½ cup whole-wheat pastry flour
(see Note)

½ teaspoon salt
¼ pound (1 stick) chilled unsalted
butter, cut into bits
2 egg yolks plus enough ice water
to make ½ cup liquid

Toast the sesame seeds in a dry skillet over medium heat, shaking
the pan so that they don't burn. When they are golden brown,
remove the pan from the heat and set it aside to cool. In a mixing
bowl or the work bowl of a food processor blend the flours with
the salt and the sesame seeds. Add the bits of butter and quickly
blend them in until the mixture is mealy (like pastry making). Add
the egg-yolk and ice-water mixture and blend in rapidly. Place a
long piece of wax paper on your work surface. With a spatula,
scrape the mixture from the bowl and spread it lengthwise on the
paper to form a strip about 10 inches or so long. Fold up the sides of
the paper and press it against the dough. With your hands shape
the dough into a roll about 1½ inches in diameter. Wrap in more
wax paper or foil and place on a cookie sheet in the refrigerator or
freezer for at least several hours.

Preheat oven to 375°F., and adjust the racks to divide the oven
into thirds. Unwrap the cracker dough. With a thin sharp knife cut
the roll into slices ⅛ inch thick. Place them 2 inches apart on
ungreased cookie sheets. Bake the crackers for 12 to 15 minutes,
until golden brown. Halfway through this baking time, reverse
the cookie sheets from the upper to the lower rack and turn them
from front to back. Remove from the cookie sheet with a spatula
and cool on a rack.

YIELD: about 6 dozen crackers
NOTE: Whole-wheat pastry flour is available in health-food stores.
You can, of course, use regular whole-wheat flour but the crackers
will not be as light.

Honey Graham Crackers

These are mildly honey-flavored crackers. Made into a sandwich with peanut butter, they make a nutritious addition to a lunch box or a satisfying after-school snack.

1¾ cups whole-wheat flour
¼ cup soy flour
2 teaspoons baking powder
½ teaspoon salt
¼ pound (1 stick) unsalted butter
¼ cup honey

¼ cup milk
1 egg, beaten with a little milk
 or water (optional)
Poppy, sesame or caraway seeds
 (optional)

Preheat oven to 375°F., and adjust the racks to divide the oven into thirds. Lightly grease 2 cookie sheets. Sift the flours with the baking powder and salt into a mixing bowl or the work bowl of a food processor. Cut the butter into small pieces and blend it into the flour until you have a crumbly mixture. Combine the honey and milk and add it to the flour to make a firm dough. Divide the dough into 4 pieces and roll each piece between 2 sheets of wax paper to about ⅛-inch thickness. You should have a rectangle approximately 6 x 8 inches. Remove the top sheet of wax paper and invert the lower sheet onto the cookie sheet, leaving room for the second rectangle of dough. Roll out the remaining pieces of dough in a similar manner. With a pizza cutter or preferably a pastry wheel with a fluted edge, and a ruler, cut the dough into 2-inch squares or rectangles 1 x 2 inches. If you like, you can brush the tops with the beaten egg and sprinkle them with poppy, sesame, or caraway seeds.

Bake the crackers for 12 to 15 minutes, or until lightly browned. Halfway through this baking time, reverse the cookie sheets from the upper to the lower rack and turn them from front to back. Transfer to a rack to cool.

YIELD: 48 squares, 2-inch size, or 96 rectangles, 1 x 2 inches

Caraway Blue-Cheese Snaps

These are a bit different from the usual cheese rounds, and they're nice to have on hand. The unbaked dough log will keep in the freezer for months.

¼ pound (1 stick) unsalted butter
¼ pound blue cheese

1 cup sifted all-purpose flour
1 Tablespoon caraway seeds

Cream the butter with the blue cheese. Add flour and knead lightly. Turn the dough out onto wax paper and form a log 1½ to 2 inches in diameter and about 8 inches long. Wrap the log in wax paper or foil and chill, preferably overnight, until dough is stiff enough to slice.

Preheat oven to 350°F., and adjust the racks to divide the oven into thirds. Cut the log crosswise into slices ⅛ to ¼ inch thick, and place slices on ungreased baking sheets. Sprinkle them with the caraway seeds. Bake for about 15 minutes, or until the edges have browned lightly. After about 8 minutes, reverse the sheets from the upper to the lower rack and turn them from front to back. Remove immediately from the baking sheets and cool on wire racks. Store in an airtight container.

YIELD: 50 rounds

Pauline's Pletzell

Pauline Blagman is a delightful octogenarian, a superb cook, and the mother of Sylvia Syms, the well-known jazz singer. Once you've tasted these, you'll know why they're her daughter's favorite.

1 large onion (8 ounces)
4 to 4¼ cups sifted all-purpose
  flour
2 teaspoons baking powder
½ teaspoon salt

¼ to ½ teaspoon freshly ground
  black pepper
½ cup vegetable oil
2 eggs, well beaten
½ cup water
2 to 3 teaspoons poppy seeds

Preheat oven to 350°F., and adjust the racks to divide the oven into thirds. Butter 2 baking sheets, or line them with foil. Chop the onion fine, but don't mince it; you don't want it watery. Sift 4 cups of the flour before measuring and resift it with the baking powder, salt and pepper. Reserve remaining ¼ cup flour. Stir the vegetable oil into the 4 cups flour. Beat the eggs and combine them with the water. Add this to the flour and oil mixture. Stir in the chopped onion and poppy seeds. Turn the dough out on a lightly floured surface and knead it briefly until soft and smooth. If it is sticky, knead in some of the reserved flour. The dough should form a soft ball.

Divide the dough into thirds and roll out each portion separately between 2 sheets of wax paper or on a floured surface with a lightly floured rolling pin. Roll it to ¼- to ½-inch thickness (see Note). Using a cutter, or floured glass, cut rounds 2 or 3 inches in diameter (see Note). Place the rounds on the baking sheets, pricking each one well with the tines of a fork.

Bake rounds for 22 to 25 minutes, or until golden brown. After about 15 minutes, reverse the sheets from the upper to the lower rack and turn them from front to back. Serve warm, if possible. Transfer to a rack to cool.

YIELD: 36 rounds, 2-inch size and ½ inch thick, or 72 rounds, ¼ inch thick
NOTE: Mrs. Blagman makes these ½ inch thick and 3 inches in diameter. I rather like them ¼ inch thick and 2 inches in diameter. They are delicious either way.

Cheese Meringues

Crisp and light, these disappear fast when served. Fortunately they are low in calories.

3 egg whites, at room temperature
⅛ teaspoon cream of tartar
1 cup grated cheese (Parmesan or Cheddar)

½ teaspoon dry mustard
Pinch of cayenne pepper (optional)
3 Tablespoons all-purpose flour
¼ teaspoon baking powder

Preheat oven to 325°F., and adjust the racks to divide the oven into thirds. Butter and flour 2 cookie sheets and set them aside. Beat 2 egg whites until they start to foam. Add the cream of tartar and beat until the whites are stiff but not dry. Combine the cheese with the remaining egg white, mustard, cayenne, flour and baking powder and mix well. Fold one fourth of the beaten egg whites into the cheese mixture to lighten it. Fold in the rest of the egg whites gently, combining everything and trying not to deflate the mixture too much. Using a teaspoon and a small rubber spatula or second spoon, drop the mixture by rounded spoonfuls onto the prepared cookie sheets.

Bake for 20 to 25 minutes, or until the meringues are barely colored.

YIELD: 50 meringues
VARIATION: Fold in ½ cup chopped nuts or toasted soybeans.

Cheddar Rounds I

This should be in everyone's repertoire. It's an old favorite that deserves its popularity. These are made like refrigerator cookies, formed into a log, and chilled for several hours before slicing and baking. They're great to have on hand (unbaked) in the freezer.

1 cup sifted all-purpose flour
½ teaspoon salt
½ pound sharp Cheddar cheese
¼ pound (1 stick) unsalted butter

⅛ to ¼ teaspoon cayenne pepper (depending on how hot you want them)

Sift the flour before measuring and resift it with the salt and cayenne. Grate the cheese very fine (a food processor is great for this). Cream the butter until soft and blend in the grated cheese. When thoroughly mixed, gradually add the sifted dry ingredients and beat until completely incorporated. Turn the dough out on a lightly floured surface. With lightly floured hands, form the dough into a round, oval or square log, about 8 inches long and 1¾ to 2 inches in diameter. Wrap the dough in wax paper or plastic and chill for several hours. Dough can remain in the refrigerator for several days. For longer storage, place in the freezer; thaw partially before attempting to slice it.

Preheat oven to 350°F., and adjust the racks to divide the oven into thirds. With a thin sharp knife, cut the chilled dough crosswise into slices ⅛ to ¼ inch thick. Place the slices on ungreased baking sheets about 1½ inches apart. Bake the crackers for 12 to 15 minutes, or until lightly colored. After about 8 minutes, reverse the sheets from the upper to the lower racks, and turn them from front to back. Loosen the crackers on the sheets and transfer them immediately to racks to cool.

YIELD: 60 rounds
VARIATION: Before baking, sprinkle the tops of the rounds with caraway seeds, toasted sesame seeds, etc.

Cheddar Rounds II

These have more of a pastry texture than Cheddar Rounds I; the cuminseeds add an interesting taste.

1 cup sifted all-purpose flour
½ teaspoon salt
¼ teaspoon white pepper
¼ pound very sharp Cheddar
  cheese

¼ pound (1 stick) unsalted butter
1 egg yolk, well beaten
2 Tablespoons whole cuminseeds

Sift the flour before measuring and resift it with the salt and pepper. Grate the cheese very fine (a food processor is great for this). Cream the butter with the cheese and work them together well. When mixed, gradually add the sifted dry ingredients and beat in the egg yolk. Turn the dough out on a lightly floured surface. Flour your hands and form the dough into a round, oval or square log about 8 inches in diameter. Wrap in wax paper or plastic and refrigerate for several hours.

Preheat the oven to 350°F., and adjust the racks to divide the oven into thirds. With a thin sharp knife cut the chilled dough crosswise into slices ⅛ to ¼ inch thick. Place them about 2 inches apart on the unbuttered cookie sheets and sprinkle them with the cuminseeds. Bake for 12 to 16 minutes, or until lightly colored. After about 8 minutes, reverse the sheets from the upper to the lower racks and turn them from front to back. Loosen the crackers on the sheets and transfer them immediately to racks to cool.

YIELD: 48 rounds

Cornbread Wafers

This slightly different form of cornbread is very nice served at Sunday brunch, or with predinner drinks.

1 cup cornmeal
1 teaspoon salt
1½ teaspoons sugar
¼ teaspoon finely ground pepper,
  preferably white

2½ Tablespoons soft butter or
  bacon drippings
1½ cups boiling water
1 egg, well beaten

Preheat oven to 400°F., and adjust the racks to divide the oven into thirds. Grease 2 baking sheets with clarified butter or vegetable shortening, or line them with foil, and place them in the oven to heat. Combine the cornmeal with salt, sugar and pepper and stir in the soft butter. Pour the boiling water over the mixture and stir until it is smooth. Add the egg and beat well. Remove the hot baking sheets from the oven. Using a spoon and a rubber spatula, place level teaspoons of the batter about 1½ inches apart on the baking sheet. Flatten them lightly with the back of a spoon.

Bake wafers for 15 to 18 minutes, until they are crisp and the edges have browned. After about 10 minutes, reverse the baking sheets from the upper to the lower racks and turn them from front to back. These are best served warm, after a brief cooling on a rack.

YIELD: 40 wafers

Poppy Seed Crackers

These are adapted from a Hungarian cookie recipe. They are thin, crunchy, and packed with poppy seeds.

1¼ cups sifted all-purpose flour
1 teaspoon baking powder
1 teaspoon salt
½ teaspoon dry mustard

¼ pound (1 stick) unsalted butter
2 Tablespoons granulated sugar
½ cup milk
5 ounces poppy seeds (1 cup)

Sift the flour and resift it with the baking powder, salt and dry mustard. Cream the butter with the sugar until soft and creamy. Gradually beat in the sifted dry ingredients and the milk, alternately. Stir in the poppy seeds, mixing them in well. Scrape the dough onto a long sheet of wax paper and wrap it well. Refrigerate it until it is just firm enough to form into a log about 12 inches long and 1½ inches in diameter. Refrigerate or freeze the log until it is firm enough to slice.

Preheat oven to 350°F., and adjust the racks to divide the oven into thirds. Butter 2 cookie sheets, or line them with foil. Remove the chilled log from the refrigerator. Using a thin sharp knife, cut the log crosswise into ¼-inch slices. Place the slices about 1 inch apart on the prepared cookie sheets. Bake for 18 to 20 minutes, until the edges are lightly browned. After about 12 minutes, reverse the cookie sheets from the upper to the lower racks and turn them from front to back. Transfer to a rack to cool.

YIELD: 48 crackers

Sources

Williams Sonoma
576 Sutter Street
San Francisco, CA 94102

The Pottery Barn
  has locations in
  California at:
1541-9 East Valley Parkway
Escondido, CA 92027

7611 Girard Avenue
La Jolla, CA 92037

10250 Santa Monica Boulevard
Century City, CA 90067

10914 Kinross Avenue
Westwood, CA 90024

4729 Alla Road
Marina Del Rey, CA 90291

110 South Hope Avenue
Santa Barbara, CA 93105

13938 Riverside Drive
Sherman Oaks, CA 91423

3525 Carson Boulevard
Del Amo Fashion Square
Torrance, CA 91367

6100 Topanga Canyon Boulevard
Woodland Hills, CA 91367

The Silo
Upland Road
New Milford, CT 06776

The Pottery Barn
  has locations in
  Connecticut at:
Civic Center Shops
Hartford, CT 06103

1205 High Ridge Road
Stamford, CT 06905

Kitchen Bazaar
4455 Connecticut Ave. N.W.
Washington, DC 20008

Wilton Enterprises
833 West 115 Street
Chicago, IL 60643

The Crate & Barrel
  has stores in Illinois at:
1510 North Wells
Chicago, IL 60610

850 North Michigan Avenue
Chicago, IL 60611

1240 Northbrook Court
Northbrook, IL 60062

54 Center Mall
Oakbrook, IL 60521

J106 Woodfield Mall
Schaumberg, IL 60195

515 Hawthorn Center
Vernon Hills, IL 60060

1515 North Sheridan Road
Wilmette, IL 60091

Cross Imports, Inc.
210 Hanover Street
Boston, MA 02113

The Crate & Barrel
has stores in
Massachusetts at:
140 Faneuil Hall Marketplace
Boston, MA 02109

171 Huron Avenue
Cambridge, MA 02138

48 Brattle Street
Cambridge, MA 02138

1045 Massachusetts Avenue
Cambridge, MA 02138

The Mall at Chestnut Hill
Chestnut Hill, MA 02167

The Store Ltd.
The Village of Cross Keys
5100 Falls Road
Balitmore, MD 21210

Kitchen Glamor, Inc.,
has stores at:
26770 Grand River
Detroit, MI 48240

1256 Great Oaks
Rochester, MI 48063

Maid of Scandinavia Co.
3244 Raleigh Avenue
Minneapolis, MN 55416

The Pottery Barn
has branches in
New Jersey at:
The Market Place
Cherry Hill, NJ 08003

Riverside Square
Hackensack, NJ 07601

The Market Place
Route 34
Matawan, NJ 07747

The Market Place
RFD 4, Route 27
Princeton, NJ 08540

The Mall at Short Hills
Short Hills, NJ 07078

The Wooden Spoon
Route 6
Mahopac, NY 10541

The Pottery Barn
has stores in
New York at:
231 Tenth Avenue
New York, NY 10011
(Main store; accepts
mail orders)

2107 Broadway
New York, NY 10023

49 Greenwich Avenue
New York, NY 10014

1292 Lexington Avenue
New York, NY 10028

117 East 59 Street
New York, NY 10022

Americana Shopping Center
2076 Northern Boulevard
Manhasset, Long Island, NY 11030

Bazaar de la Cuisine
1103 Second Avenue
New York, NY 10022

Bridge Company
214 East 52 Street
New York, NY 10022

Manhattan Ad Hoc Housewares
842 Lexington Avenue
New York, NY 10021

Paprika Weiss
1546 Second Avenue
New York, NY 10028

H. Roth
1577 First Avenue
New York, NY 10022

Both Paprika Weiss and H. Roth are excellent sources of spices, flavorings and flours as well as of baking equipment. Roth also sells apricot and prune lekvar and fresh almond paste.

Cake Decorators
2892 Johnstown Road
Columbus, OH 43219

One Potato, Two Potato
5115 Carlisle Pike
Mechanicsburg, PA 17055

The Pottery Barn
has two locations
in Pennsylvania:
Suburban Square
Ardmore, PA 19003

1610 Chestnut Street
Philadelphia, PA 19103

The House on the Hill
South Strafford, VT 05070

Vermont Country Store
Weston, VT 05161

Custom cookie sheets
can be ordered from the
following two stores.
Unfortunately, neither accepts
mail orders.

Bob Michaels Surplus Corp.
323 Canal Street
New York, NY 10013

Space Surplus Metals
325 Church Street
New York, NY 10013

Index

Alice's Stove-Top Date Nut
Balls, 76
Almond(s)
Basler Leckerli (Swiss
Honey Drops), 189
Christmas Almond Wafers,
177
Chinese Almond Cookies,
86
Chocolate Almond
Meringue Bars, 133
Chocolate Chips, 58
Coconut Almond Bars, 152
Ginger Almond Bars, 161
Gingersnaps, 99
Lena's Almond Biscotti,
204
Paste, 13; *also see* Note,
135
South Dakota Almond
Cookies, 105
Spritz Almond Cookies,
198
Squares, 141
Tacos, 31
Tiles (Tuiles), 36
to blanch, 13
to cut or shred, 13
to store, 13
Aluminum foil, 3
Anise, aniseeds, 22
Cookies, 96
oil, *see* Note, 203
Toast, 203
Apple, Applesause
Applesause Walnut Bars,
142
Apple Whole-Wheat
Drops, 35
Oatmeal Applesauce
Cookies, 70
Apricot Bars, 143
Apricot Filling, 167
Arrowroot, *see* Note, 39
Arrowroot Wafers, 36

Baking powder, 13
Banana Spice Drops, 40
Bars and Squares, 140–174
Almond Squares, 141
Applesauce Walnut Bars,
142
Apricot Bars, 143
Brownies, 144
Brownies, Katharine

Hepburn's, 145
Butterfudge Fingers, 148
Butterscotch Brownies, 146
Chocolate Almond
Meringue Bars, 133
Chocolate Chip Nut
Bars, 150
Chocolate Nut Bars, 151
Christmas Fruit Squares,
179
Christmas Squares,
Yugoslavian, 188
Cocoa Brownies, 147
Coconut Almond Bars, 152
Coconut Pecan Bars, 153
Date Nut Bars I, 154;
II, 156
Duxbury Cheesecake
Squares, 157
Foxy Fruit Bars, 158
Ginger Almond Bars, 161
Heavenly Bars, Lois's, 163
Lemon Bars, 162
Meringue Nut Bars, 132
Newton Twins, 164
Oatmeal Raisin Squares,
168
patting out batter by
hand, 27
Peanut-Butter Oatmeal
Bars, 169
Pecan Raspberry Bars, 170
Prune Nut Bars, 171
Raisin Squares, Old-
Fashioned, Gerta's, 160
Seedcake Bars, 172
Toffee Bars, 173
Zucchini Walnut Bars, 174
Basler Leckerli (Swiss
Honey Drops), 189
Benne Seed Wafers, 44
Black Pepper Cookies, 106
Black Walnut Cookies, 85
Blagman, Pauline, 218
Blender, 5
Blueberry Meringues, *see*
Variation, 129
Brandy Snaps, English, 65
Brownies, 144
Butterscotch, 146
Cocoa, 147
Katharine Hepburn's, 145
Butter, 14; to clarify, 14
Butter Cookies, Mexican, 80
Butterfudge Fingers, 148

Butterscotch
Brownies, 146
Chocolate Chips, 59
Coconut Fingers, 77
Cookies, 95
Caramel Nut Cookies, 102
Caraway, Caraway Seeds, 22
Blue-Cheese Snaps, 217
Rounds, 100
Rye Crackers, 206
Seedcake Bars, 172
Cardamom, *see* introductory
note, 78
Cardamom Coconut Wafers,
78
Carrot Lemon Drops, 41
Castine Raisin Cookies, 116
Cats' Tongues, 123
Cheddar Rounds I, 220;
II, 221
Cheese
Caraway Blue-Cheese
Rounds, 217
Cheddar Rounds I, 220;
II, 221
Duxbury Cheesecake
Squares, 157
Filling, 157
Meringues, 219
Onion Cheese Crackers,
211
Peruvian Parmesan
Pennies, 212
Chinese Almond Cookies, 86
Chocolate, 14
Almond Chocolate Chips,
58
Almond Meringue Bars,
133
bits or morsels, 15
Brownies, 144
Brownies, Katharine
Hepburn's, 145
Butterfudge Fingers, 148
Butterscotch Chocolate
Chips, 59
Chocolate-Chip Cookies,
60
Chocolate-Chip Nut
Bars, 150
Chocolate Chunk Cookies,
67
Chocolate Coconut
Macaroons, 136
Chocolate Cookies, 95